VOLLEYBALL DRILL BOOK:

Individual Skills

Bob Bertucci

NTC/Contemporary Publishing Group

Library of Congress Cataloging-in-Publication Data

Bertucci, Bob.
Volleyball drill book: individual skills / Bob Bertucci.
p.   cm.
ISBN 0-940279-28-2
1. Volleyball—training.   I. Title.
GV1015.5.T73B48   1992
796.325—dc20   92-9540
                                                                          CIP

Cover design by Jim Beever
Text design by Leah Marckel
Diagrams by Julie Biddle

Published by Masters Press
A division of NTC/Contemporary Publishing Group, Inc.
4255 West Touhy Avenue, Lincolnwood (Chicago), Illinois 60712-1975 U.S.A.
Printed in the United States of America
International Standard Book Number: 0-940279-28-2
          03 04 05 RCP 22 21 20 19 18 17 16 15 14 13 12 11 10 9 8 7

INTRODUCTION

Volleyball Drill Book: Individual Skills has been developed to help coaches and teachers provide a progressive method of teaching young volleyball athletes. Each of the seven chapters focuses on a separate skill, and the drills are sequenced so that they gradually increase in difficulty and relevance to game situations.

Before you turn to the actual drills, I will explain how to design a drill so that you can better understand and use these drills, while hopefully stimulating your imagination to create your own.

Each drill should have an objective that is fully understood by the players. Ask yourself: How do I improve a skill? What is the most effective way to accomplish this? You then need to address the training variables and understand the impact of each variable.

The four drill variables are **type**, **quantity**, **quality**, and **intensity**.

Type of the drill refers to movement. Is the drill static or dynamic? Does the drill address skill mechanics or game action? Is it a game sequence or simulation drill? Quantity has to do with the duration of the drill and the number of contacts. Quality is the degree of perfection or proficiency required. Intensity is the time interval between each exercise. For example, if very little time is allowed between contacts and the length and number of contacts in a drill is high, the drill is physically demanding. The more quality required, the more skill is needed. The more dynamic the drill, the more relevance it has to the actual game.

If you experience difficulties with a drill, consider the following:

1. The number of balls, nets, and special equipment needed.

2. The number of players needed in the drill.
   a) How many active learners?
   b) How many non-active learners (shaggers)?

3. Physical conditioning of the athletes.

4. Skill level of the athletes.

5. Mental and emotional level of the athletes.
   a) Level of concentration needed.
   b) Frustration and/or boredom factor.
   c) Is the drill goal oriented, competitive, or game-like?

Drills can be categorized in many ways, one example would be **coach-oriented** or **player-oriented**. In the coach-oriented drill, the coach is the center of the action. This enables the coach to manipulate some training variables directly. These drills can be effective for a skilled coach, especially if the players lack skills. However, a program of too many coach-oriented drills should be avoided, because it reduces the role of the players. In player- oriented drills, the players perform the drills by themselves. The coach's primary duty is to supervise.

A second way to categorize drills is by the difficulty and number of skills practiced within a drill, an example using this method are the categories of: **simple**, **combination**, and **complex**.

The simple drill is one repetition of one skill or multiple repetitions of one skill. Simple drills are addressed extensively in this book and are very effective for teaching volleyball fundamentals. At higher levels of play, simple drills should be used in pre-season training and as warm-up exercises.

Combination drills are repetitions of two or more skills not in succession. These drills enable players to practice a number of different skills, and provide some degree of application to the game.

The complex drill is a repetition of two or more skills performed in succession. Complex drills have the most application to the game and should always be designed with a game sequence in mind.

Drills can also be categorized by the number of participants: **individual drills**, **small group drills**, and **team drills**.

All of these categories, variables, and considerations are part of developing a well rounded training program. Variety is important in maximizing the drills in any book. The coach's ability to be creative in selecting and designing drills is critical to a well trained team.

Good Luck and Success in training your team.

TABLE OF CONTENTS

VOLLEYBALL DRILL BOOK: INDIVIDUAL SKILLS

KEY TO DIAGRAMS

⟶	Path of Player
- - -▶	Path of Ball
◯	Player
⬭ (dashed)	Player's New Position
●	Setter / Target
Ⓧ	Coach
⌐	Chair
▭	Ball Cart
[▭ with oval]	Basket
◖	Hoop
Ⓢh	Shagger
△	Cone

CHAPTER 1

PASSING DRILLS

1 THREE-STEP PASS DRILL

Objective: To teach basic passing skills, while stressing body, arm, and hand position.

Description: Players work in pairs, facing each other about 15′-20′ apart.

Step #1 Player A tosses the ball high in the air towards player B. B moves under the ball and lets the ball land on the finger tips. After the ball rebounds from B's hands, the ball is retrieved and tossed back to A. Player A then lets the ball rebound from the hands, retrieves the ball, and continues the drill. The key phrase in the first step should be "squat under the ball."

Step #2 Player A tosses the ball to player B. B sets the ball straight up, catches the ball, and tosses the ball high in the air back to A. Player A then sets the ball straight up, catches the ball, and continues the drill. In the second step, the key phrase is "Basket over the Forehead."

Step #3 Player A tosses the ball to player B. B makes a direct pass back to A. Player A then returns the pass directly to B, and the drill continues. It is important that the pass be made at least 12′ high so that both players will have an opportunity to move under the ball to make the pass. The third step's key is "Extend."

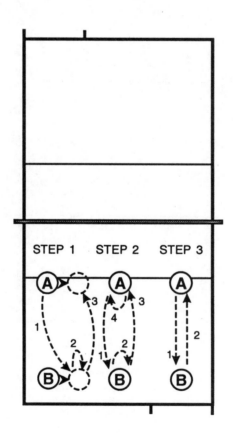

2 RAPID FIRE PASSING DRILL

Objective: To develop overhead passing skills.

Description: Players form two lines as shown in the diagram below. Tossers (A) stand side by side in one line, and passers (B) are in another facing the tossers. Additional players rotate into the passing line. All tossers have a ball. The drill is initiated by having the tossers toss underhand to the players in front of them. The passers position their hands, assume proper position, and set the ball back to the tosser using an overhead pass. After setting the ball, they move to their right, stop, and receive another toss until they reach the last tosser. The player then moves to the end of the passing line.

Variation: Use an underhand pass.

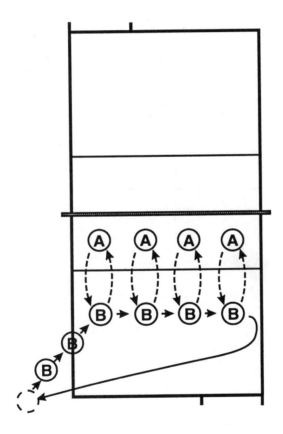

3 CHAIR DRILL

Objective: To work on accuracy and low trajectory in passing concentration.

Description: Players designated as tossers are positioned on chairs near the net (A). Receivers (B) are positioned across the court at the attack line (station 1). The tossers toss easy balls to the receivers, who attempt to pass the ball back over the net and into the tossers' raised hands. The drill continues with receivers spending one minute at each of the three stations shown in the diagram. After three minutes the tossers and receivers switch positions and perform the drill again.

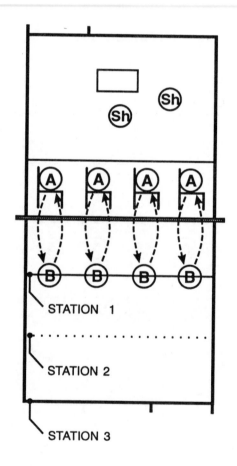

STATION 1

STATION 2

STATION 3

4 HIT THE WALL TARGET DRILL

Objective: To develop accuracy in passing.

Description: A target is placed on the wall at a height above eight feet. Players form a single line facing the target with the first player in line about 5′ from the wall. Player A passes the ball to the wall five times, attempting to hit the target each time. After the five passes, A then goes to the end of the line, and the next player repeats the process until everyone has had an opportunity. Score (accuracy in hitting the target) can be kept to make this a competitive drill.

Variation: The players line up in two lines in front of a wall. The first player in one line sets the ball up to the wall and then runs to the end of the line. The first player in the other line then plays the ball and runs to the end of the line. The rotation continues as players play the ball to the wall.

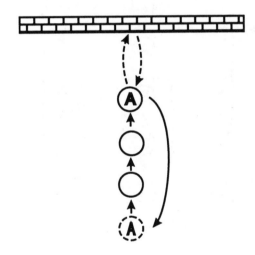

5 WALL RELAY DRILL

Objective: To develop passing skills and ball control.

Description: The players divide into three lines facing a wall, as illustrated below. On command, player A in each of the three lines self-passes the ball, passes the ball against the wall, and goes to the rear of the same line. The second player in the line (B) then moves up and, from the rebound off the wall, passes the ball against the wall and goes to the rear of the same line.

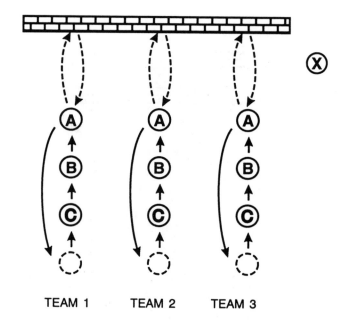

TEAM 1   TEAM 2   TEAM 3

        INDIVIDUAL SKILLS

6 LINE REBOUND WALL PASS DRILL

Objective: To teach elementary passing skills and develop proper body position and movement skill.

Description: Players form two lines next to each other and facing a wall as shown in the diagram below. The first player in the line on the left (line A) passes to the wall and goes to the end of the opposite line (line B) . The first player in line B takes the rebound, passes the ball back to the wall, and then goes to the end of line A. The drill continues until everyone has had a chance to participate in both lines.

Variation: To simplify this drill, the coach can allow the rebound to bounce on the floor before the next player passes.

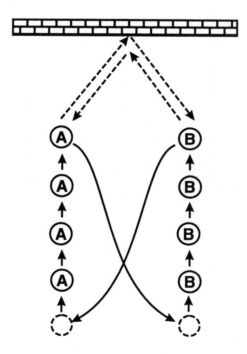

7 VOLLEY-BASKETBALL DRILL

Objective: To develop proper movement and skill technique for the over-head pass.

Description: Two players stand near each other and face a stationary hoop that is approximately 10′ high. Player A begins by tossing or passing the ball to player B, who sets the ball into the hoop. This drill provides an excellent means for evaluating the accuracy of players' overhead passes.It is also a good means of creating competition between individuals or teams of individuals.

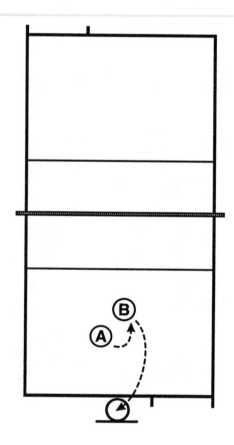

8 CONTINUOUS PASSING DRILL

Objective: To develop ball control.

Description: Players work individually, bumping the ball to themselves using a one-hand or a two-hand bump pass and continuing to pass the ball to themselves for a specific amount of time or number of passes.

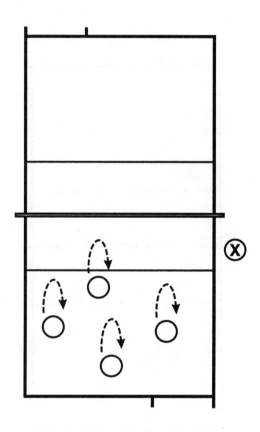

9 PASS BUMP PASS DRILL

Objective: To develop passing skills and ball control.

Description: Players work in pairs. Player A makes a low pass to player
B, (1) who self-bumps the ball straight up (2). B then passes the ball back
low to A (3), who also self-bumps the ball (4) and continues the drill.

Variation: Use all overhand passes, make the self-pass an overhand pass.

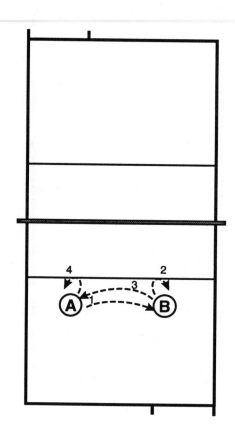

INDIVIDUAL SKILLS

10 MOVING PASS DRILL

Objective: To develop efficient movement and visual tracking of the ball.

Description: Players work in pairs facing each other. Players A and B pass the ball back and forth while moving in a circular fashion as shown in the diagram below. Player A sets or overhand passes the ball, and player B bump passes or underhand passes the ball.

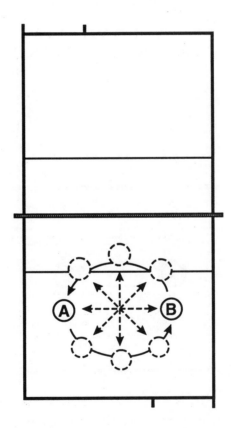

11 PIVOT AND PASS DRILL

Objective: To develop the ability to turn and make an accurate pass.

Description: Players work in pairs. Player A tosses the ball high in the air (1) and then passes the ball high to player B (2). B makes a complete turn (3) and returns a high pass back to A (4), who also makes a complete pivot (5). This drill continues until one player misses a pass.

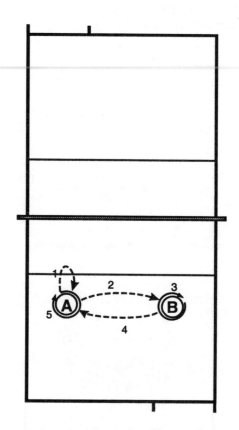

12 MOVE AND TOSS DRILL

Objective: To review underhand passing skill, introduce passing for service reception.

Description: This drill requires four players--two tossers, one receiver and one player positioned as if in the center-front position of a W service reception formation. Switching between the right-back (#1) and the left-back (#5) positions, the receiver (A) returns tosses from the two designated tossers (B). The center player (C) practices opening up towards the receiver and adding support, similar to the actions required of that position in a game.

Variation: The difficulty of the drill can be increased by having the tosser switch to serving the ball to the receiver instead of tossing it, while the other player positions close to the net like a setter.

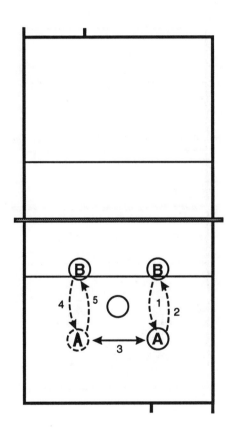

13 WARM-UP PASSING DRILL

Objective: To use as a warm-up drill, and to develop ball control and proper footwork.

Description: Player A passes to B (1). A immediately sprints to touch a line or spot on the floor (2) and then sprints back to original position (3). B passes the ball back to A (4), and mirrors the movements of player A (5,6.)

Variations:

1. Have the players use either overhand or underhand passing.

2. Increase the distance the players must move.

3. Use lines already in place on the court.

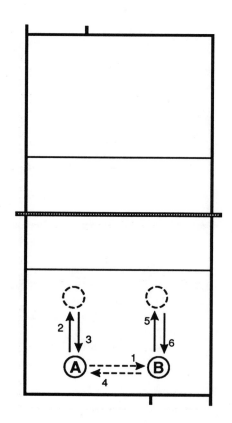

14 UNDER THE NET DRILL

Objective: To practice forward and backward movement and to develop passing accuracy.

Description: The drill is done in pairs. The tosser (A) starts the drill by slapping the ball, which signals the passer (B) to move toward the tosser in a low comfortable position (1). As soon as B moves under the net, A passes the ball to B (2), who underhand passes the ball to A (3) and returns to the original position (4). The drill can be done continuously for a specified amount of time.

Variations:

1. Use overhand pass instead of underhand pass.

2. Have the tosser make a self-pass before passing to the moving player.

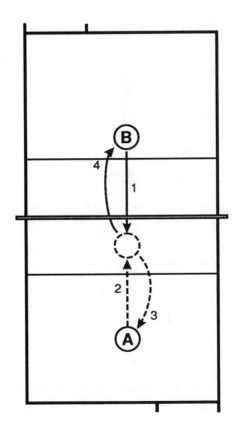

15 UNDER AND OVER THE NET DRILL

Objective: To improve passing and proper movement.

Description: Player A slaps the ball to initiate the drill, signalling B to start moving towards A (1). Once B crosses under the net, A passes the ball to B (2), who in turn passes the ball back to A (3). Then B returns to the starting position (4). As B is returning, A passes the ball over the net (5) for B to pass again (6).

Variation: Both the underhand and overhand pass can be used.

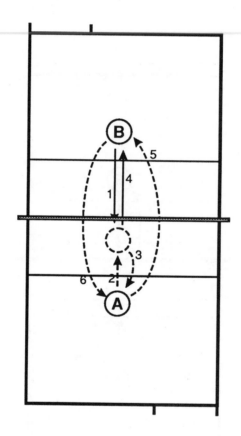

16 PARALLEL LINE PASS DRILL

Objective: To develop basic passing skills and movement awareness.

Description: After forming two parallel rows about 10′ apart, the players work in pairs, passing a ball back and forth. At the command of the coach, who calls out "High," "Low," "Forward," or "Back," one parallel line of players moves forward or backward accordingly to pass the ball. For the first pass, for example, the A players could pass the first ball high. The coach could then call "Back," to the B players who would execute a deeper pass, forcing the A players to backpeddle to move into a position to pass.

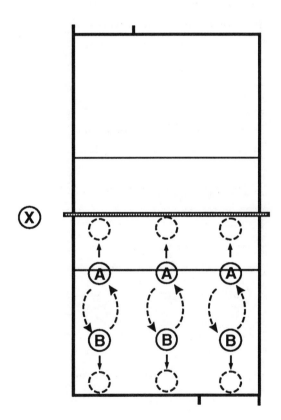

17 RUN AND SET DRILL

Objective: To increase passing skill after movement, positioning in passing, and angle of pass.

Description: Players work in pairs, positioned approximately 20′ apart. Player A starts the drill by setting the ball to player B (1),then runs forward (2) to receive the ball directly in front of player B (3). Player A then sets the ball back to B (4) and back pedals to the starting position (5). As A is returning to the starting position, B sets the ball back to A (6) and the drill is repeated. When player A has finished, B will switch positions with A.

Variation: Use an underhand pass in performing drill.

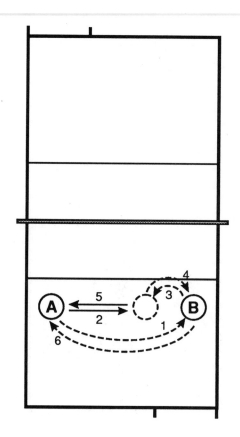

INDIVIDUAL SKILLS

18 RUN, CIRCLE, AND SET DRILL

Objective: To increase setting skills and movement efficiency.

Description: Players work in pairs positioned approximately 20′ apart. Player A starts by setting a ball to player B (1). After the ball is set, A runs towards B (2). B sets the ball back to A (3). A sets to B (4) and circles around B (5) while B self-sets the ball (6). When A finishes the rotation, B sets the ball back to A (7). A sets to B (8) and backpedals to the starting position (9), where B sets again (10) to continue the drill.

Variation: Continue the drill with B running toward A after the set, at which time the sequence is done in reverse.

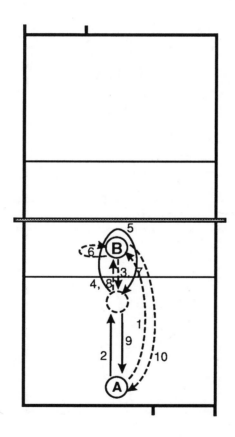

19 SETTING STRENGTH DRILL

Objective: To develop passing control and setting strength.

Description: Two players start opposite each other on the baselines. Player A sets the ball to the closest attack line (1), runs under the ball (2), sets it over the net to Player B on the opposite baseline (3), then returns to the starting position (4). B sets to the closest attack line (5), runs under the ball (6), sets it to A on the opposite baseline (7), then returns to starting position (8). Player A continues the drill by repeating the same sequence.

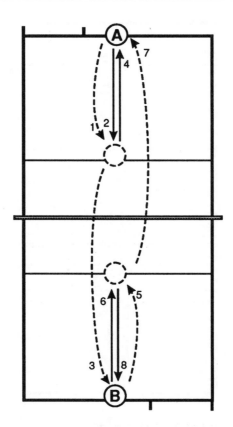

20 ONE-ON-ONE DRILL

Objective: To develop passing skills.

Description: Two players are standing on opposite sides of the net and pass a ball back and forth over the net, restricting their movements to an area of approximately 10′ by 10′. This can be accomplished by using an extra set of net antennas. If played as a competitive drill, one point is given to a player if the other player is unable to pass the ball over the net or misses the pass.

Variations:

1. Players can be allowed five passes each while moving down the net, while their partners follow.

2. Players pass near the net and then move one step backward after each pass until one player cannot pass over the net.

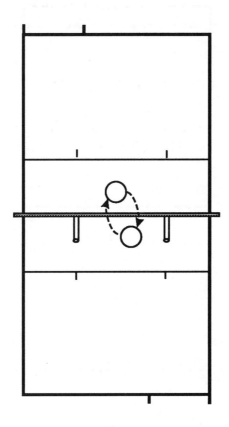

21 ONE OUT PASS DRILL

Objective: To develop basic passing skills and movement efficiency.

Description: The players form a single line as shown below. Player A passes the ball to player B, who passes it back to A and then goes to the end of the line. A then passes the ball to the next person in line (C) and the drill continues.

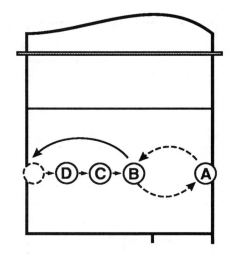

22 LINE-TO-LINE PASS DRILL

Objective: To develop basic passing skills.

Description: The players form two lines, shown in the diagram as lines A and B. The first player in line A passes to the first player in line B (1) and goes to the end of line A. The first player in line B then passes to the (new) first player in line A and goes to the end of the B line. The drill continues in the same manner until everyone has had a chance to pass the ball.

Variation: Players participating in the drill can be required to use a specific type of pass, for example, the jump set (jump in the air and make an overhand pass) or the bump pass.

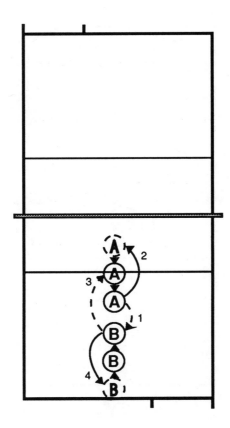

23 THREE-PERSON LINE DRILL

Objective: To develop proper passing skills and conditioning of the players.

Description: This drill is performed in groups of three. The drill is initiated by player A passing the ball to player B (1). A then follows the pass and moves behind player B (2). As soon as A begins to move, C steps up to take A's place. (3) Player B then passes the ball to C (4) and follows the pass by moving behind C (5). Always start the ball on the side that two players are located.

Variation: Both the overhand and the underhand pass can be used.

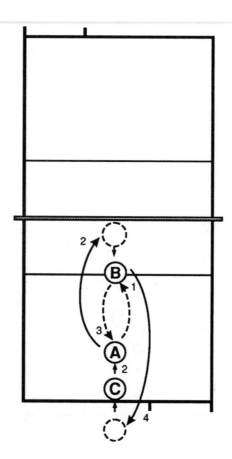

INDIVIDUAL SKILLS

24 THREE-PERSON AGILITY PASSING DRILL

Objective: To develop passing skills.

Description: Three players stand in line about 10′ apart from each other. Player A tosses or passes to player B (1), who immediately makes a full (360 degrees) turn (2) and executes a backward pass to player C (3). Player C then makes a high pass to A (4), who turns 180 degrees (5) and passes the ball back to B (6). At this point, play is halted. All players rotate counter clockwise, and the drill begins again.

Variation: Continue the drill without stopping.

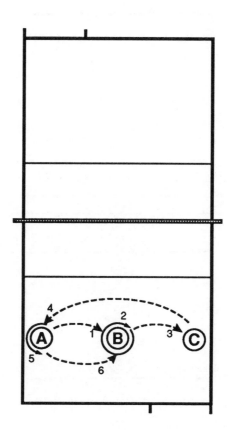

25 UNDERHAND BUMP PASS DRILL

Objective: To learn control of the underhand bump pass.

Description: The players form a single line. The first player in line (A) tosses the ball and bumps it forward a few feet, about 12′ high (1,2). A then hits sets forward (3), runs under the ball (4), makes an underhand bump pass (5), runs under the ball (6), pivots 180 degrees (7), and then bumps the ball to the next player in line (B). This player repeats each step, and the drill continues.

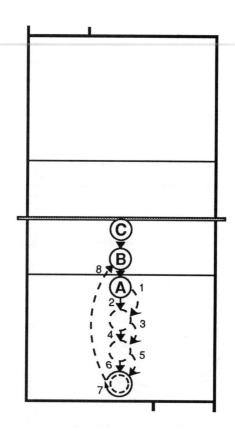

INDIVIDUAL SKILLS

26 KEEP IT IN PLAY DRILL

Objective: To develop ball control and communication.

Description: Three receivers start about 5′ apart as shown in the diagram below. The coach starts with two balls and tosses the first ball to any of the receivers (1). The receiver then passes the ball to one of the other receivers (2). Before the first ball is returned, the coach tosses the second ball (3). Players try to keep both balls in play, using controlled passing (4,5,6).

Variation: Have the players pass the ball immediately back to the coach.

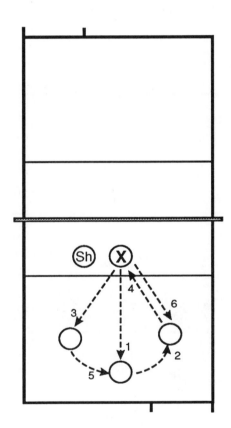

27 BACK SET ROTATION DRILL

Objective: To develop the ability to skillfully execute the over-the-head pass.

Description: Players form lines of three with the first player (player A) facing the other two.

Step #1 Player A passes the ball to B (1) and moves to assume B's place in line (2), but facing C. B back sets to C (3) and then moves to A's former position (4).

Step #2 Player C passes to A (1), A backsets to B (2). Then B and C exchange positions (3).

Step #3 Player C passes the ball to A (1) and assumes A's place in line facing B (2). A backsets to B (3) and then moves to C's position (4).

Variation: This drill can be performed without any players exchanging positions; the middle player would simply turn and back set.

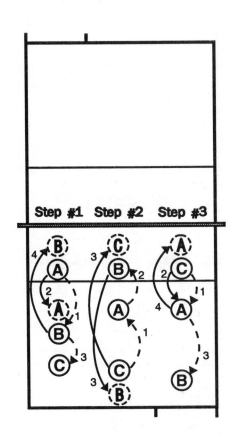

28 TOSS AND PASS DRILL

Objective: To develop passing skills.

Description: Players line up next to each other facing the coach. The coach tosses the ball to player A. A passes the ball back to the coach. The coach then passes the ball to the next player, making corrections as needed, until every player has handled the ball.

Variation: The coach can increase the difficulty of the drill by requiring the player to back pedal and touch the baseline immediately following each pass.

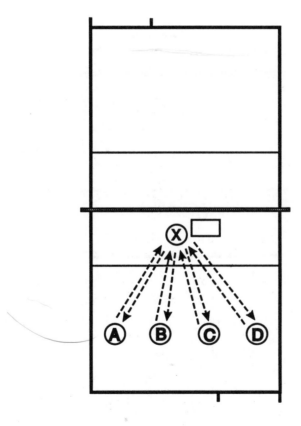

29 SET AND SWITCH DRILL

Objective: To practice setting and lateral movement.

Description: Two players are positioned opposite the coach as shown in the diagram below. The coach has two balls, and begins the drill by tossing one ball to player A (1). While A is setting back to the coach (3), the coach quickly tosses another ball to player B (2), who also sets back to the coach (4). As soon as a player sets the ball back to the coach, the player switches to the other player's position (5,6).

Variation: Use the underhand pass.

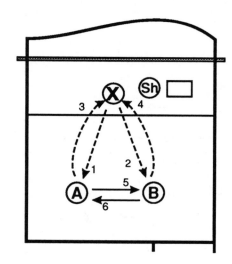

30 BOUNCE AND RECOVER DRILL

Objective: To develop the ability to quickly recover from the floor and to move and play the ball.

Description: A target is positioned next to the coach near the net. Receiver A is positioned in the left-back (#5) position. Additional players line up behind the baseline behind A. The first receiver assumes a stomach-down position. When the coach bounces the ball on the floor (1), the receiver must get up, run to the ball (2), and pass the ball to the target before it bounces again (3). The target shags the ball and places it in the ball cart (4) and returns to the end of the line (5). The receiver then rotates to become the target.

Variations:

1. Vary the degree of difficulty by varying where the ball is bounced.

2. Vary the position of the coach or the players.

3. Use either overhand or underhand passing.

4. Vary the target.

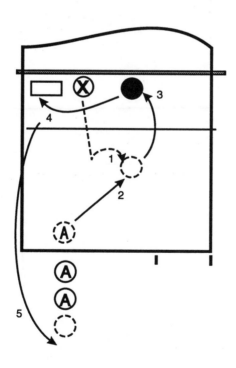

31 UP AND BACK SETTING DRILL

Objective: To develop movement efficiency and increase passing accuracy.

Description: Three players are positioned behind the baseline and the coach about mid-court. The coach tosses the ball to the right-back (#1) position (1). Player A moves under the ball from the baseline (2) and sets to the target (3).A backpeddles to the original position (4), as B begins to move in and set the next ball which is tossed to the center-back (#6) position. C completes the sequence, moving into the left-back (#5) position as soon as B sets the ball. When C sets the ball, A is ready to begin the drill again.

Variations:

1. Require the players to back pedal to a wall or a point behind the baseline.

2. Use the underhand passing technique.

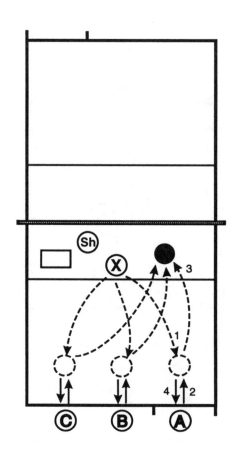

32 AROUND THE WORLD PASSING DRILL

Objective: To develop passing skills and ball control.

Description: The players form a single line facing the coach and a designated target. The coach serves or tosses the ball in the vicinity of player A (1). Player A moves to meet the ball (2) and then passes the ball toward the target (3). A then runs around an obstacle which has been placed on the court and returns to the end of the original line(4).

Variation: To create competition in this drill, the coach can specify a number of consecutive times that the target must be hit. If a player misses the target, the count goes back to 0.

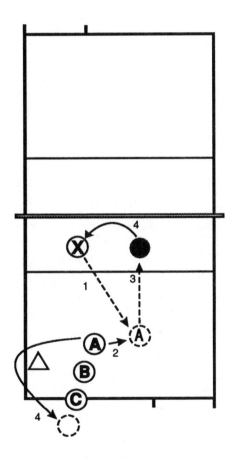

33 INTO THE BASKET DRILL

Objective: To develop passing accuracy.

Description: Three players (A,B,C) form a triangle approximately 15'-20'
  apart with additional players lined up behind player B and a basket
  positioned near player C. Player A begins the drill by throwing the ball
  to player B (1). This throw represents the serve. B then passes the ball
  to the basket (2). Player C shags the ball (3). Each person rotates: A goes
  to the end of line B, B replaces C, and C replaces A (4).

Variation: Player A could be positioned on the opposite side of the net,
  simulating a serve over the net.

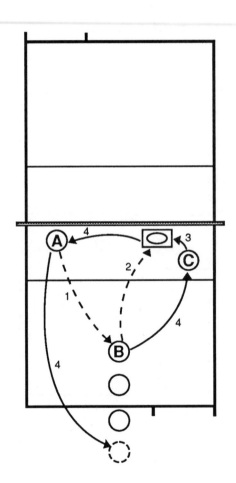

34 DIG AND SET DRILL

Objective: To develop basic digging and setting skills.

Description: Three players are positioned on the court as shown in the diagram. The coach either throws or hits the ball to player A in the back court (1), who digs the ball to player B positioned to the right (2). B takes the dig pass and sets the ball cross-court to player C at the net (3). C catches the ball and returns it to the coach (4). All players rotate one position to the left and the drill continues. If more than three players are participating in the drill, the extra players line up behind the setter (B). When the group rotates, the player at the net (C) receiving the set goes to the end of the setter's line.

Variations:

1. Have the player receiving the set spike the ball across the net.

2. The drill can be done continuously and to both sides.

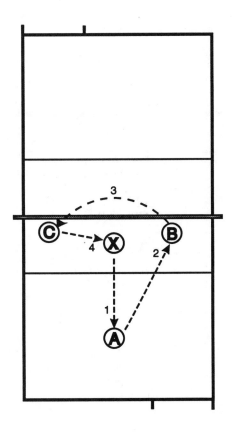

35 HIT THE TARGET DRILL

Objective: To develop basic passing skills and ball control.

Description: The players form two lines facing the coach and the target, as shown in the diagram. The coach serves or tosses the ball to player A (1). A bumps the ball to the target (2) and then moves to the end of the line (3). Player B retrieves the ball (4) and gives it back to the coach (5).

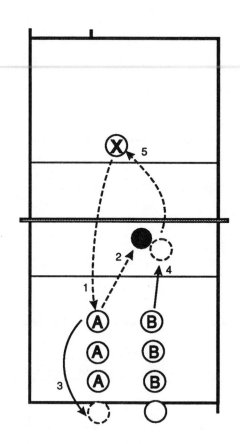

36 FREE BALL PROFICIENCY DRILL

Objective: To increase proficiency of both the left and the right-back positions in free ball passing.

Description: Two players are positioned to receive the ball across the court from the coach. Another player is designated as the target and is positioned near the net. Additional players are lined up behind the target and to the rear of each receiver, behind the base line. The coach throws or hits balls over the net, alternating to either side of the court (1). The player in the line closest to the ball passes it to the target (2) and goes to the end of the target line (3). Each target person audibly counts the running total of perfect passes. The target shags the ball, crosses under the net (4), hands the ball to the coach and goes to the end of a receiver line (5).

Variations:

1. Allow only overhand passing to be used.

2. Increase the difficulty of the free balls by not hitting them near the passing line.

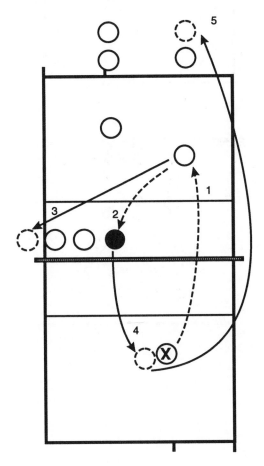

37 PRETZEL DRILL

Objective: to promote passing accuracy, proper movement and teamwork.

Description: The coach starts the drill by tossing a ball to player A in the left-back (#5) position (1), who passes the ball to the target (2) and immediately switches positions with player C in the center-front (#3) position (3). The coach then tosses a ball to player B in the right-back (#1) position (4). B passes the ball to the target (5). B immediately switches with player A (6). The coach then tosses the ball to C in the #5 position (1), and the drill is repeated again.

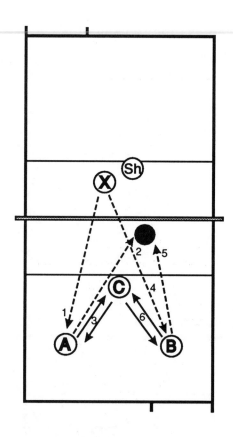

INDIVIDUAL SKILLS

38 ON-THE-MOVE ROTATION PASSING DRILL

Objective: To develop basic passing skills and ball control.

Description: The players form a single line facing the coach. Two players position themselves near the net in the right-front (#2) position, player B, and left-front (#4) position, player C. The coach throws or tosses the ball to the first person in line, player A (1), who then passes the ball to B (2). B then passes the ball to C (3). C catches the ball and gives it back to the coach(4). The players rotate clockwise with B going to the end of the line (5), and the drill continues.

Variation: A specific kind of pass (underhand bump, overhead set) could be required at each position.

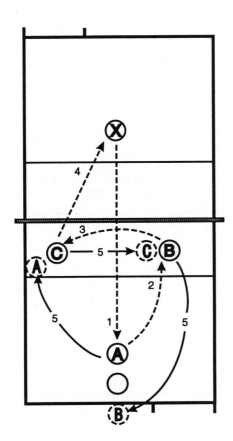

39 BASKET RELAY DRILL

Objective: To develop accurate overhead passing techniques.

Description: Players form a line approximately 15'-20' away from the coach as shown in the diagram below. A single player is positioned on the attack line as the setter. The coach throws the ball, varying the speed, to the first player in line (1). This throw represents the serve. The player who receives the throw then makes a bump or underhand pass (representing the service reception) to the setter (2). The setter then passes the ball (representing the set) into the basket (3). After passing the ball into the basket, the setter then retrieves the ball for the coach (4) and moves to the end of the line in which the first player stood (5). The first player then replaces the setter, and the drill continues.

Variation: Move the basket either to the center or the right-front position.

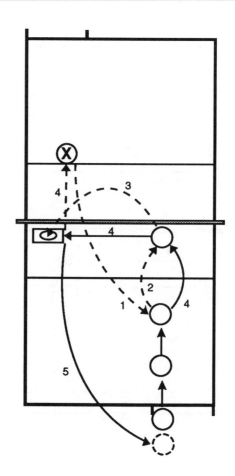

INDIVIDUAL SKILLS

40 PRECISION BUMP PASS DRILL

Objective: To develop bump pass accuracy.

Description: Two receiving players are positioned across the net from a line of players who will bump pass to either of them. The coach tosses the ball to the first player in line (1), who bump passes the ball to the receiver indicated by the coach's command at the toss (2). After the bump pass, the passing player goes to the end of the line (3). The receiving player immediately bump passes the ball to the coach (4).

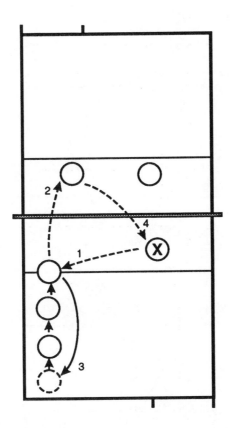

41 PASSING CIRCUIT DRILL

Objective: To develop speed and range.

Description: Players line up behind the baseline opposite the coach, and two targets position themselves on either side of the net as show in the diagram. The coach throws a ball short to the right-front (#2) position (1). The first player (A) sprints (2) and plays the ball with a roll up to the first target (3). A then sprints under the net to the left-back (#5) position on the other side of the court (4). The coach immediately spikes to that position (5) and the player digs the spike to the second target (6). A then sprints back under the net to the opposite left-back (#5) position (7) and plays a thrown ball from the coach to the first target (8). The drill can be repeated or A can go to the end of the line.

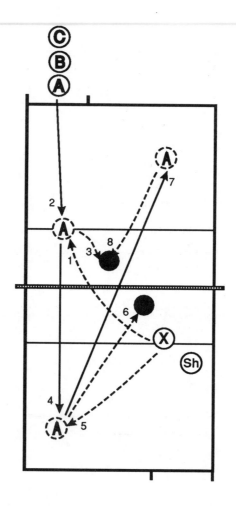

INDIVIDUAL SKILLS

42 TRIANGLE PASS DRILL

Objective: To develop basic passing skills and movement efficiency.

Description: Three players form a triangle facing each other with at least one additional player lined up behind the player at the head of the triangle (player A). Player A passes to B (1) and then takes B's position (2). B passes to C (3) and assumes C's position (4). C then passes the ball to the next person in line (5), now in A's original position, and goes to the end of the line.

Variation: If more than one triangle is used, this drill can involve competition between the groups.

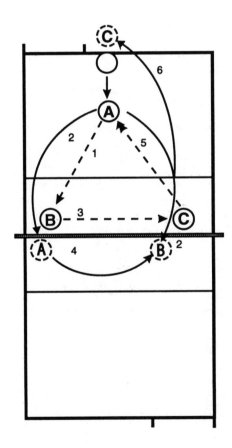

43 T-PASS DRILL

Objective: To develop passing accuracy and control.

Description: Players line up in a "T" formation as pictured below. The first player in the line (A) begins the drill by passing the ball to the center-front (#3) position player B (1). After passing, A will immmediately move to the end of the passing line. B then faces the player in the right-front (#2) position (C) and passes the ball (2). C then passes the ball over B to D in the left-front (#4) position (3). D then passes the ball to player E who has replaced player A (4).

Variation: The middle player can execute a back set to the #2 position player.

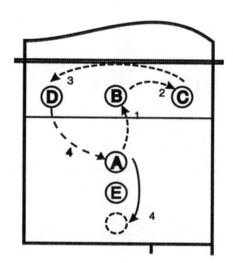

INDIVIDUAL SKILLS

44 BOX DRILL

Objective: To develop overhand/forearm passing accuracy and communication.

Description: Four players set up in a box formation. The two players closest to the net each have a ball (A and B). These players simultaneously pass straight across (1), and the receivers (C & D) return the ball (2). A and B then pass diagonally (3), and the receivers again return the ball (4).

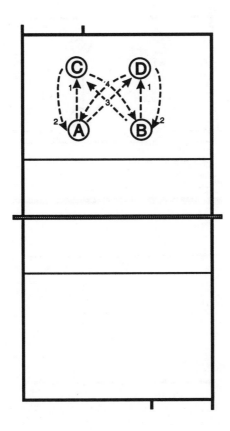

45 PASS AND SWITCH DRILL

Objective: To develop movement and setting skills.

Description: Four players form a rectangle as shown in the diagram. Player A sets to player B (1) and, after setting, switches places with player C (2). B sets to C, who is now at A's original position (3), then B switches with player D (4). C sets to D and the drill continues.

Variation: Use an underhand pass.

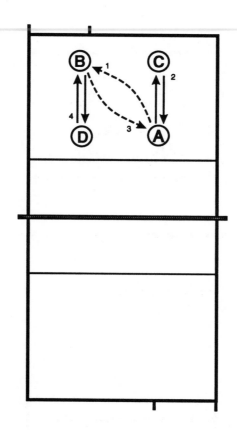

46   LATERAL BOX DRILL

Objective: To develop lateral movement, footwork, and passing accuracy.

Description: Four players set up in a box formation, the two players nearest the net each having a ball. The players nearest the net (A) simultaneously pass to the two players farthest from the net (1), then move laterally and switch positions with each other (2). The players farthest from the net (B) return the pass (3) and also move laterally and switch positions with each other (4), and the drill continues.

Variation: Use either underhand or overhand passing.

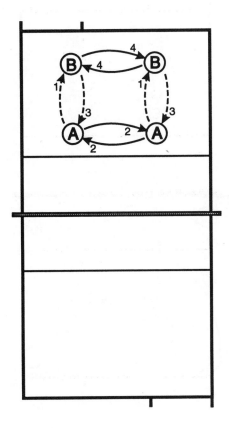

47 FOUR CORNERS DRILL

Objective: To improve passing skill and movement efficiency.

Description: The players form four lines behind the four corners of a square. After each player passes the ball, the player follows the pass and goes to the end of that line. The direction of the passes should be made as illustrated to ensure an orderly flow.

Variation: Put two balls into play.

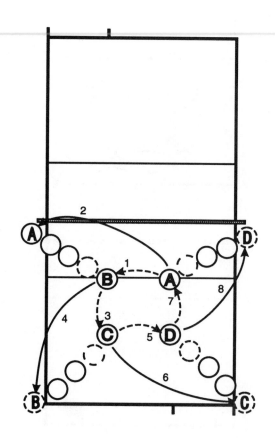

INDIVIDUAL SKILLS

48 MULTIPLE LINE PASSING DRILL

Objective: To develop basic passing and movement skills.

Description: The players form four lines as illustrated in the diagram. Each line is approximately 15′ from the opposite line facing it. Two balls are used. The two lines running the length of the court pass the ball back and forth to each other using high passes. The two lines running the width of the court pass the ball back and forth to each other using low passes. After each pass, the player making the pass rotates to the end of the line on the right.

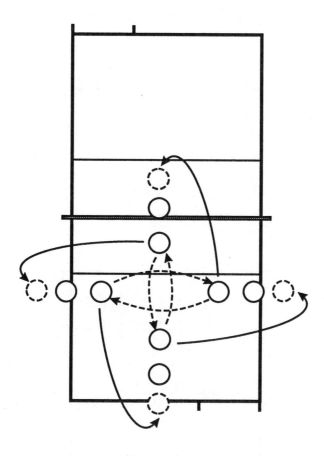

49 ANGLING THE PLATFORM DRILL

Objective: To develop basic passing skills and the concept of angling the passing platform.

Description: Players form two lines facing each other. The first player in the line near the net (A) begins by tossing or passing the ball to the first player in the opposite line (B), who angles a pass across to the next player in the first line. The players continue passing the ball, alternating a straight pass and an angled pass, to the next player in the opposite line. Players in the line closer to the net always pass straight while the players closer to the baseline angle the pass. A missed pass is returned to the player who missed it, and the drill is restarted from that point.

Variation: The drill can continue back to the starting point by the players closer to the baseline angling their passes to the left.

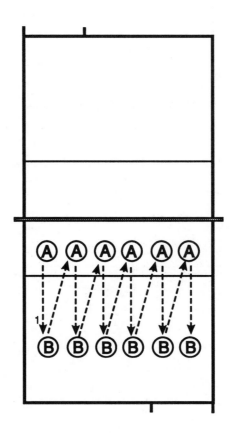

INDIVIDUAL SKILLS

50 LINE-TO-ONE PASS DRILL

Objective: To develop basic passing skills, ball control, and teamwork.

Description: The players line up in a semi-circle with one player (player A) facing the group. Player A starts the drill by passing the ball to player B at the left end of the semi-circle (1). A immediately follows the pass and lines up to the left of B (2), while player G moves into A's former position (3). B passes the ball to G (4). The drill continues with players moving in a semi-circular formation.

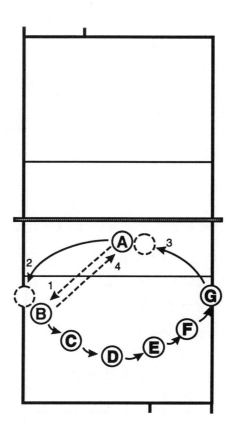

51 STAR DRILL

Objective: To improve passing accuracy, ball control, and team unity.

Description: The players form the shape of a star, as illustrated. Using one ball, a player at any point on the star passes the ball to an adjacent player, who in turn passes it to the next player, and so on. Every player is encouraged to face the player receiving the pass.

Variations:

1. More than one ball can be used.

2. The balls can be started at different points on the star.

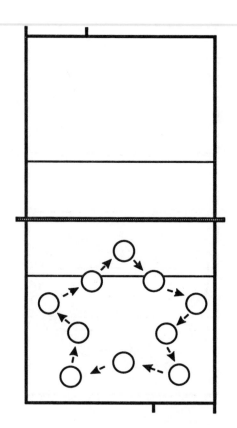

52   CIRCLE CROSS DRILL

Objective: To improve passing accuracy, ball control, and team work.

Description: The players form a circle as illustrated in the diagram. Using one ball, Player A passes to adjacent player B (1). B then passes to the player opposite, C, (2). Following two basic rules--"a ball from around on the right always should be passed across" and "a ball from across should always be passed to the individual on your left"--the drill becomes fairly simple to perform. One complete revolution of the drill involves eight separate passes.

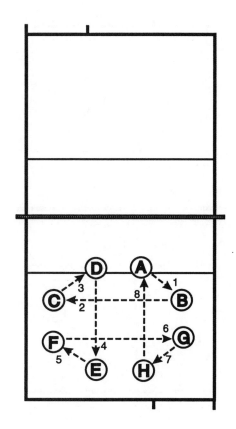

53 FACE AWAY CIRCLE PASS DRILL

Objective: To develop passing skills and ball control.

Description: The players form a circle with their backs turned away from a player positioned in the middle. The player in the middle calls out a specific player's name as the ball is passed to that player (1), who turns (2) and tries to return the pass to the player in the center (3). If that player misses the pass, the player is then required to face the center of the circle and is ineligible to participate until all the players have missed.

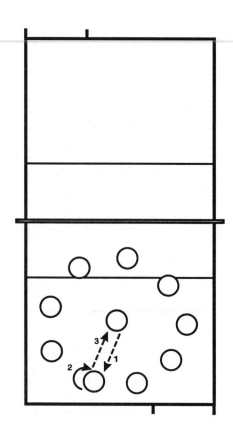

INDIVIDUAL SKILLS

54 KEEP IT GOING DRILL

Objective: To develop basic passing skills and ball control.

Description: The players form a circle and use one ball for this drill. All the players begin to slowly jog around the circle. Player A passes or tosses the ball straight up, and the next player (B), while continuing to run in the circle, reaches the ball and passes it straight up again. Each player in the circle does the same thing. The group tries to keep the ball in the air as long as possible while continuing to run.

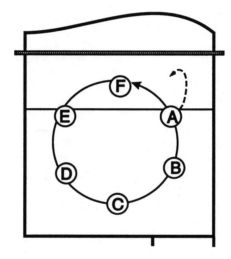

55 CIRCLE ROTATION PASS DRILL

Objective: To develop basic passing skills and movement skills.

Description: The players form a circle with player A in the middle. A begins by passing the ball to player B who passes the ball back to the player A. A proceeds to consecutively pass to each player in the circle while facing that player. Another player will replace A in the middle when every player in the circle has received a pass.

Variation: Don't use a player in the middle of the circle, simply keep the ball moving around, across, or in any direction of the circle to any player, using overhand or underhand passes.

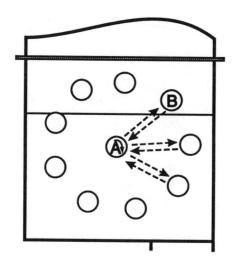

INDIVIDUAL SKILLS

56 CLOCK DRILL

Objective: To improve passing accuracy and passing technique.

Description: One player stands in the center of an imaginary clock. Additional players are lined up behind the 12 o'clock position. The player in the center passes to the first player in line. The first player returns the pass and moves to the 9 o'clock position, receives and returns a pass there, and then does the same at the 6 o'clock and the 3 o'clock positions. After moving around the clock, the player goes to the end of the line.

Variation: Use the overhand pass or digging a spiked ball.

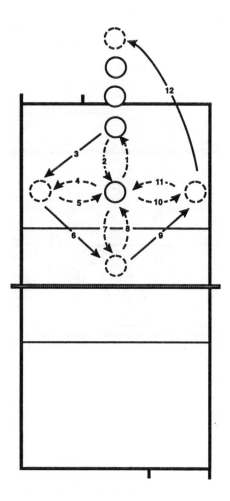

57 MY CALL, YOUR PASS DRILL

Objective: To develop squatting under the ball and movement efficiency.

Description: Players are assigned letters and stand in a circle around one player, who begins the drill by calling out one of the player's letters and passing the ball up into the air. The player in the center takes the place of the player whose letter was called as that player comes to the center and also passes the ball straight up. The new player in the center of the circle then calls another number and the process is repeated.

Variation: Use this drill employing the underhand pass to develop the concept of angling the platform.

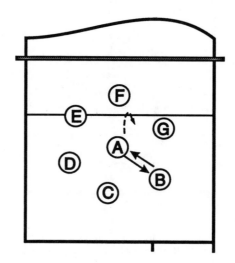

58 TWO-PERSON CIRCLE DRILL

Objective: To improve passing accuracy and movement efficiency.

Description: The players form a circle with players A & B positioned in the center. Two balls are used. Both A & B pass to someone opposite in the perimeter of the circle, in the diagram C & D (1). The player receiving the pass then passes the ball back to the player who made the original pass (2). The players in the center then pass clockwise to the next players in the circle, E and F (3). Both center players exchange places with the players who received the first pass (4). The players now in the center will receive the pass from the perimeter player and again pass it clockwise before exchanging positions.

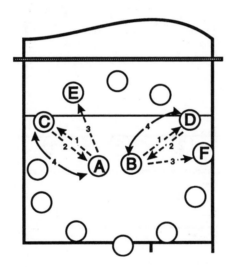

59 CALL-THE-NUMBER PASS DRILL

Objective: To develop passing skills and mental acuity.

Description: Each player is numbered according to position. The coach tosses the ball to a player and calls out a number. The player receiving the toss must then pass the ball to the player whose number was called.

Variations:

1. This drill can be used by placing the players in a circle and using the players' names instead of numbers.

2. A game called H O R S E may also be played. If a player misses passing to a number, or misses the pass completely, the player is given a letter (H O R S E in order). If the player misses five times, the player is out of the game.

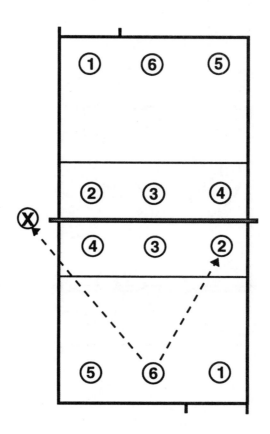

INDIVIDUAL SKILLS

60   6 ON 6 PASSING DRILL

Objective: Practice using all volleying skills in a game situation.

Description: Six players are on each side playing the game of volleyball. However, only the volleying skill of overhand and underhand passing can be utilized.

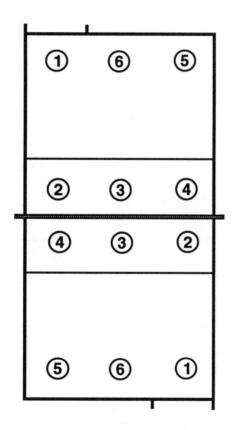

CHAPTER 2

SERVING DRILLS

61 TOSS AND CATCH DRILL

Objective: To develop a consistent service toss.

Description: Players line up behind the opposite baselines. The first player in each line holds the ball in one hand about chest high. Each of these players tries to release the ball directly in front of the hitting shoulder, one to two feet above the body, and then catch it. After five throws, the players each go to the end of the line. The formation in this drill can be altered to accommodate a larger number of players.

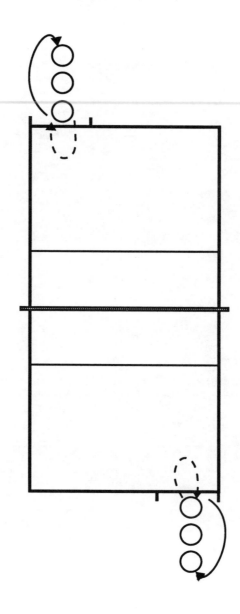

62 WALL SERVE DRILL

Objective: To develop basic mechanics of serving, especially hand contact.

Description: Players form a line 30′ from a wall which has been marked with a line the same height as the net. The player serves the ball above and as close as possible to the line. The ball bounces back to the server and is repeated.

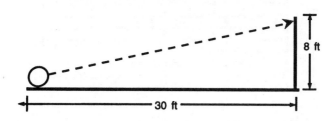

63 WALL SERVE FOR POINTS DRILL

Objective: To develop accuracy in serving.

Description: A line is drawn on a wall at net height. A 5′ square target is placed above this line inside a 10′ by 15′ rectangle, as illustrated in the diagram. The server tries to hit the target from three distances (10′, 20′, and 30′) which are marked on the floor. Each server is given a specific number of serves from each distance, and score is kept. A score of either five or ten points is awarded for hitting the specified target areas.

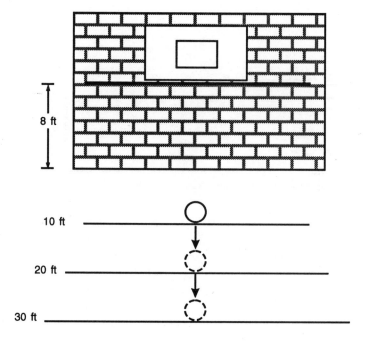

INDIVIDUAL SKILLS

64 MOCK SERVICE DRILL

Objective: To develop basic mechanics of serving.

Description: Players pair off and stand about fifteen feet apart from each other on opposite sides of the net. Player A starts the drill by executing correct serving technique and serving the ball to player B. B then returns the serve. As technique and accuracy improve, the players gradually move toward the base line until they're hitting a full serve.

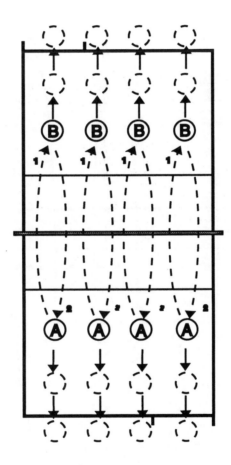

65 FULL COURT SERVING DRILL

Objective: To improve serving technique and accuracy.

Description: Three sets of partners line up on opposite base lines. One side begins by serving straight ahead to their partners (1). The partners retrieve the balls and immediately serve back (2).

Variations:

1. Tie a rope approximately two feet above the net, and have the players serve between the net and the rope.

2. Have players practice both short and long serves.

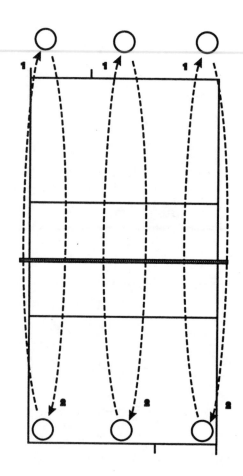

66 TWO PLAYER SERVING DRILL

Objective: To develop cross court serving proficiency.

Description: Two players stand approximately fifteen feet apart on opposite sides of the net. One player serves to the other (1). The receiving player catches the serve and then serves back to the other player (2).

Variation: Move the players farther apart as they achieve a greater level of accuracy in serving.

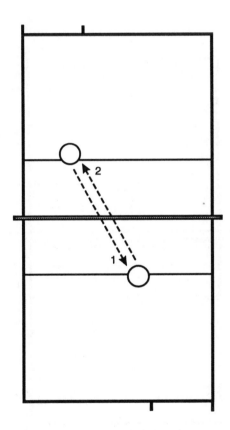

67 SERVE AND JOG DRILL

Objective: A Warm-up exercise as well as serving skill work.

Description: Players line up along the service line. The first server serves to the right-back (#1) position (1), retrieves the ball (2), and returns to the end of the line (3). As soon as the first server is out of the way, the next player steps in and also serves to position #1.

Variation: Practice serving to all six court positions.

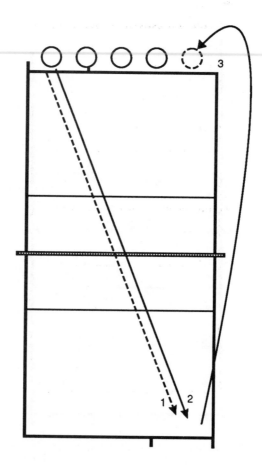

68 SERVING FOR CONSISTENCY DRILL

Objective: To develop serving accuracy and consistency.

Description: A player attempts five serves to designated areas. For every miss, the player must hit a specified number of additional serves.

Variation: Increase the number of serves required to designated areas.

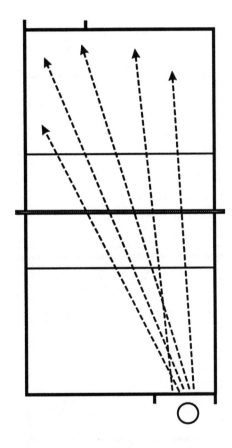

69 SPEED AND CONSISTENCY SERVING DRILL

Objective: To develop consistency and proficiency in serving.

Description: One player stands on the end line in the serving position. The other players shag balls so that the server has a constant supply. The server attempts to complete as many serves as possible within a specific one- to two-minute time limit. The coach stands near the server, timing and counting how many consecutive serves the player achieves. Once the server misses, a new player serves.

Variation: Require the server to serve to a specific area.

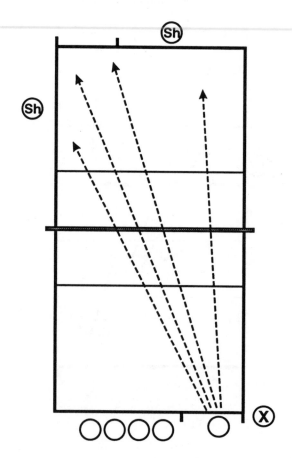

INDIVIDUAL SKILLS

70 SERVING UNDER PRESSURE DRILL

Objective: To develop serving proficiency under stressful conditions.

Description: The players are divided into two equal teams. Each player takes a turn serving a designated number of serves. The coach keeps score as the drill progresses. One point is awarded for a successful serve, and two points are taken away for a missed serve. The first team to reach fifteen points is the winner.

Variation: Serve to a predetermined area.

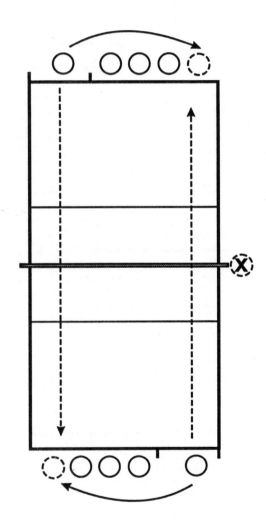

71 CUMULATIVE SERVE PRESSURE DRILL

Objective: To develop serving proficiency under stressful conditions.

Description: The coach stands at the side of the net. Players form two teams and line up on opposite end lines. Each player in turn makes one serve attempt to a designated area and then returns to the back of the line. The coach keeps a running total of how many consecutive serves each team makes within the designated area. If any player misses a serve, the entire teams total returns to zero.

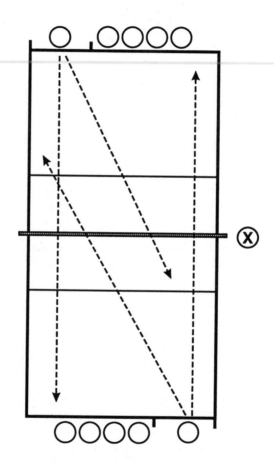

INDIVIDUAL SKILLS

72 FULL COURT TARGET PRACTICE DRILL

Objective: To develop service accuracy.

Description: Players form two lines behind the service line. Two mats or other such targets are placed in the court on the other side of the net. The lines alternate serving on command. After serving, the server goes to the end of the line. Scores may be kept by awarding points for hitting the targets.

Variation: A specific target or a specific kind of serve which must be used can be designated for each rotation of the servers.

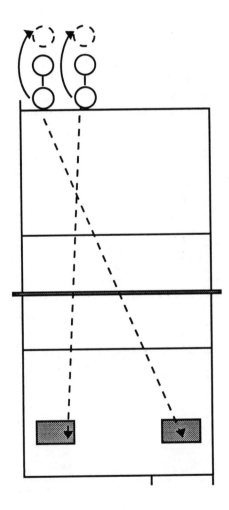

73 SERVING AT A TARGET DRILL

Objective: To develop accuracy and proper technique in serving.

Description: Players line up behind the service line. A mat is placed as a target on the opposite court. The first player in line serves the ball, attempting to hit the mat. The mat is moved to different areas of the court after a specified number of service attempts.

Variation: Begin the drill by having the player serve from mid- court position before subsequently moving to a position behind the service line.

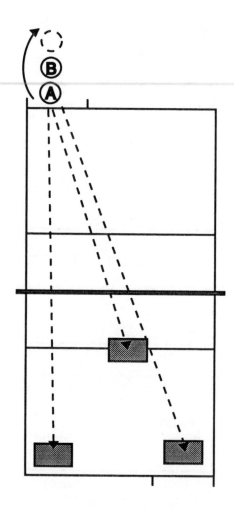

INDIVIDUAL SKILLS

74 SHORT SERVES DRILL

Objective: To develop accuracy and proper technique in serving.

Description: Three mats are placed on the court or three areas are marked off. Each server is given a specific number of serves to hit one of the three targets.

Variations:

1. Award points for hitting the target, and keep score.

2. Have the player hit one target a specific number of times before moving to the next target.

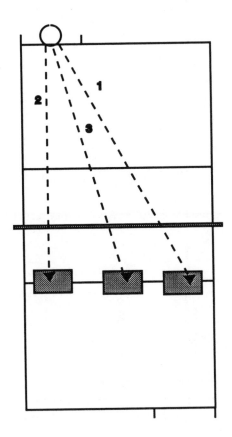

75 SERVING FOR POINTS DRILL

Objective: To develop accuracy and skill in serving.

Description: The court is marked into five "point" zones as illustrated. The zones worth four and five points are 3 ft. wide. The zone worth two points is marked 5 ft. back from the net. A player is given a specific number of serves and score is kept. The higher point total is given for a ball that lands on the line.

Variation: Divide the players into teams, with each team having the same number of serves per player.

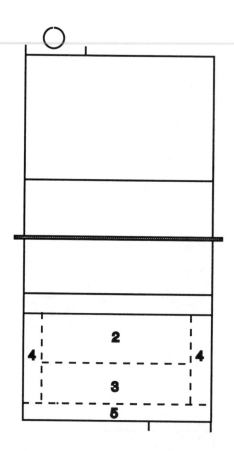

INDIVIDUAL SKILLS

76 SERVING TO SCORE DRILL

Objective: To develop accuracy and proper technique in serving.

Description: The court is marked into a grid containing nine zones with a mat placed in the center of each zone. A serve hitting the mat in any of the three farthest zones earns five points. Hitting the area in these zones, but not the mat, earns two points. Serves landing on the mats in the middle zones earn two points, with one point awarded for hitting these zones but not the mats. The closest zones earn ten points and five points, respectively, for hitting the mats or just landing in the zone.

Variation: Change the point scores so that the highest score is given either to the area most important in which to serve or to the area which needs the most improvement.

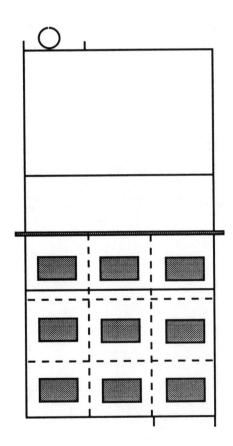

77 NINE-HOLE SERVING DRILL

Objective: To practice serving accuracy while playing a game.

Description: The court is divided up into nine holes designated by numbers placed on the court, as illustrated in diagram. The server begins by serving the ball into each area consecutively. A card is kept by each player recording the number of tries it takes to hit nine holes. Servers must retrieve their own ball each time. The number of tries are added up and the player with the least amount of serves is the winner.

Variation: Designate holes #10 through #18 on the other side of the court, and start half the team on the back nine.

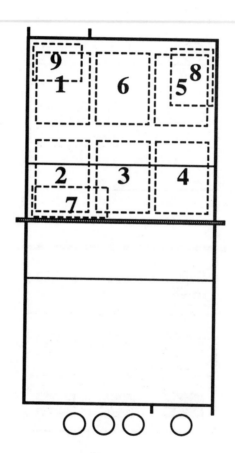

INDIVIDUAL SKILLS

78 LINE SERVE AND PASS DRILL

Objective: To develop serving accuracy.

Description: Player A hits a moderately difficult, but accurate, serve to
B (1) and then moves into the court to receive (2). B moves to take the
serve (2), self-bumps the ball (3), shags it, and then serves it back to A
(4).

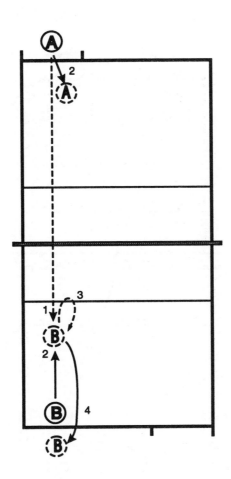

79 SERVING FOR ACCURACY DRILL

Objective: To develop serving accuracy and passing technique.

Description: The players form two lines, servers and receivers. Three of the receivers assume positions in back court. Server A calls out to one of the receivers and then serves to that player (1). The player receiving the serve self-passes the ball (2), catches it, and then rolls it back to the serving line (3). After each serve, the server rotates to the end of the serving line, and the player receiving the serve moves to the end of the receiving line (4).

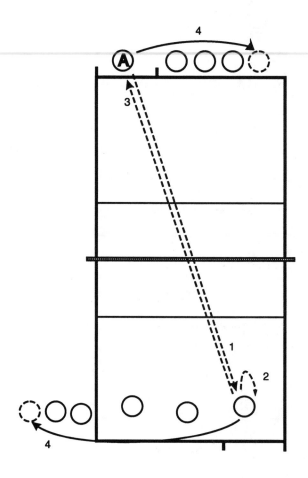

INDIVIDUAL SKILLS

80 SERVE AND BUMP DRILL

Objective: To develop serving techniques and passing ability.

Description: The players form two lines, servers and receivers. Player A stands close to the net to the right of the receiving line as a target for the receivers. B hits a ball to C (1), who then bumps the serve to A at the net (2). After the serve, B rotates to the end of the receiving line (3), C replaces A at the net (3), and A goes to the end of the serving line (3).

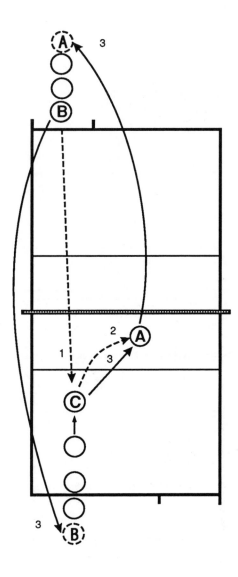

81 DRIVE SERVE DRILL

Objective: To develop a high speed low trajectory serve and to improve individual serve reception.

Description: Player A is located as receiver in the court area to which the servers most need to practice serving. Player B begins in the opposing service area. A rope/string is attached to the top of the antennaes. B must serve the ball above the net and below the antenna rope. After serving B goes immediately to the end of the serving line, and the next server (C) will serve to A. The receiver (A) will pass each ball to the target and then prepare for the next serve. Rotate the receivers after a set period of time.

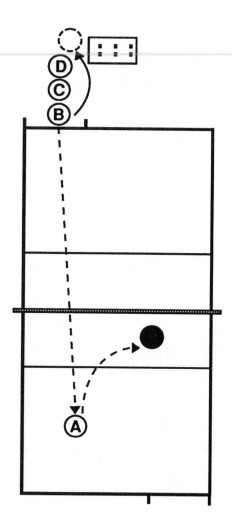

82 TWO PASSER SERVE DRILL

Objective: To develop the ability to serve against the two player receive. To improve service reception.

Description: Players A and B position themselves in a two player service reception formation. Player C is located in the service area of the opponent court. A rope/string is attached to the top of the antennaes. C will serve three balls between the net and the antenna net to the receiving team in an attempt to score an ace serve. Immediately after serving, C will go to the end of the serving line and D will prepare to serve. After a specified number of successful passes have been completed, the receivers should switch.

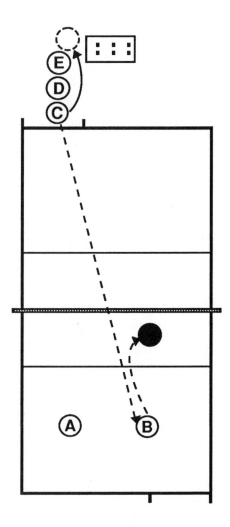

INDIVIDUAL SKILLS

CHAPTER 3
SERVICE RECEPTION DRILLS

83 BASKET PASS DRILL

Objective: To develop service reception skills.

Description: Players line up in a semi-circle facing player A. Player A tosses or passes the ball to all players, who attempt to pass the ball through a hoop or into a basket behind A as shown in the diagram below. One point is scored for each basket.

Variations:

1. Use this drill with any passing skill.

2. Have two groups compete against each other to see which group scores the highest number of points.

3. Perform this drill using a basketball goal as the target.

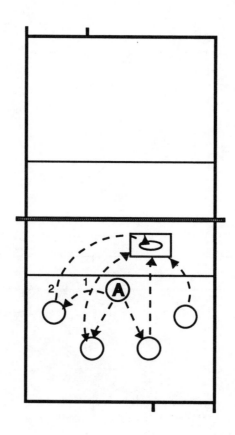

84 ACCURACY MAT PASSING DRILL

Objective: To develop accurate service reception skills.

Description: Players line up in the middle of the court opposite the coach. The coach tosses the ball to the first player in line, (1) who passes the ball to the mat (2). After five passes, the player then rotates to the end of the line (3).

Variations

1. The location of the mat can be varied.

2. The distance and the placement of the line can be varied.

3. The player receiving the serve can be required to use a specific type of pass.

4. Points can be awarded for hitting the mat and individual scores kept.

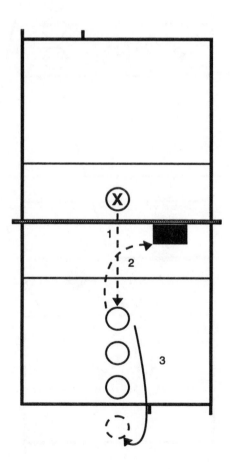

85 SPRINT AND HIT DRILL

Objective: To increase foot speed and kinesthetic awareness in service reception.

Description: The coach and the players are positioned behind the same baseline. Upon the signal of the coach, the first player sprints to the left-back (#5) position on the opposite side of the net (1). The coach serves the ball as soon as the player reaches the net (2). The receiver turns, receives the serve, and passes the ball to the designated target (3). The player then moves to the end of the line (4).

Variations:

1. Vary the positions to which the coach serves.

2. Vary the type of serve used by the coach.

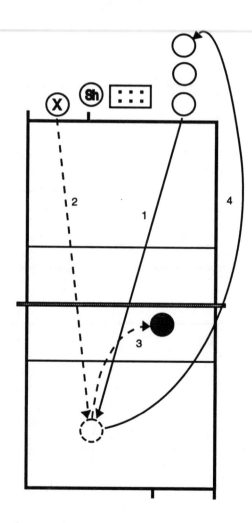

86 LATERAL MOVEMENT SERVICE RECEPTION DRILL

Objective: To improve lateral movement efficiency during the service reception.

Description: A player is positioned in the middle of the backcourt to receive the serve, and a setter is positioned near the net. The coach puts the ball in play using a medium speed serve to either side (1). The player must move to the ball quickly (2), pass the ball to the setter (3), and then return to the neutral position (4). The coach should remind the player that when passing from the left side of the court, the inside (right) shoulder should be lowered and the trunk laterally flexed to the right which should slightly drop the player's upper right side, angling the passing platform toward the target.

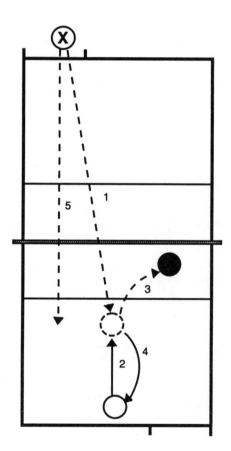

87 FORWARD MOVEMENT IN THE SERVICE RECEPTION DRILL

Objective: To improve the ability to move forward during the service reception.

Description: A receiver starts in the center-back (#6) position, assuming a ready position, and a setter or target is positioned near the net. The coach puts the ball in play, using a serve that drops in front of the receiver (1). The player moves toward the ball to receive the serve (2) and passes the ball to the setter/target (3), using a relatively low pass to assure accuracy. Immediately after the pass the receiver retreats to the #6 position (4), and the coach serves another short serve.

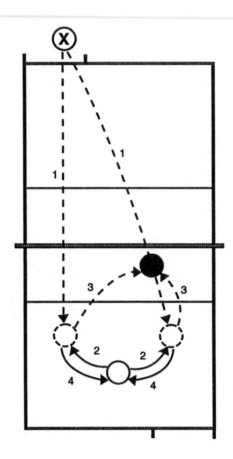

88 COMPETITION DRILL

Objective: To develop accuracy in service reception.

Description: Receiver A is positioned in the left-back area of the court. Other players line up outside the court on the left side. One player is positioned as a target at the net and one is positioned near the coach at the baseline to act as a shagger. The coach puts the ball in play from the opposite baseline, serving down the line into any area of the back one-third of the court (1). The receiver attempts to receive the serve and quickly pass it to the target (2). After each pass, the player moves one position to the right and the drill is repeated, as illustrated. One point is awarded for each pass the player accurately delivers to the target. The first player to earn 15 points wins the game. After three passes, the receiver takes the shagger's place, and the shagger moves to the end of the line.

Variations:

1. Rotate the receiving line from the right to left with the additional players lined up outside the right side of the court.

2. Start the receiving line at the net to enhance backward movement skills, or at the baseline to develop forward movement proficiency.

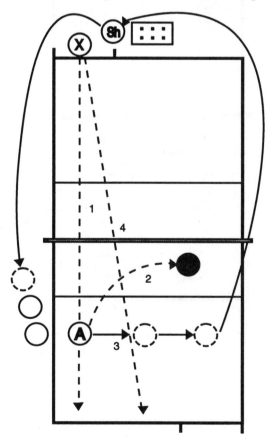

89 RAPID FIRE RECEPTION DRILL

Objective: To develop service reception skills and mental alertness.

Description: Five players are positioned in a W service reception formation with the other players lined up on the side line to be rotated in. The coach serves the ball to one of the receivers (1), who bumps the ball to a target (2). After every ball, the players immediately rotate positions (3). The coach serves rapidly and randomly.

Variation: The target could be a setter practicing and setting a particular set.

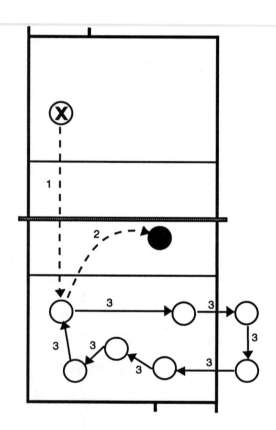

INDIVIDUAL SKILLS

90 MULTI-POSITION SERVICE RECEPTION DRILL

Objective ; To develop a player's ability to receive serves in all areas of the court.

Description: Player A is positioned in the right-back position of a W service reception formation with additional players lined up behind the baseline as shown below. As the coach serves the ball from the opposite baseline to each of the five positions of the W service reception formation, A moves to pass the ball. Each player must pass five balls in succession to the setter, one from each position, before returning to the end of the line.

Variation: Position two players in the right-front (#2) and left-front (#4) positions. The setter sets the ball to one of these players, who hits the ball to a designated area.

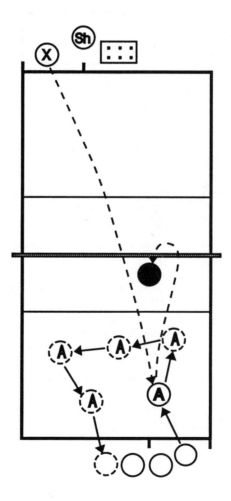

91 PASSING ACCURACY DRILL

Objective: To develop accuracy and precision in passing skills.

Description: Three receivers are positioned parallel to the baseline. The coach puts the ball in play from a platform on the opposite side of the net (1), using a variety of directions, speeds, spins, trajectories, etc. The receivers must accurately pass the ball to a setter (2) who catches the ball. If the setter is able to maintain proper foot placement, the receiver is awarded one point. A receiver must accumulate a predetermined number of points before moving to the next position.

Variations:

1. Have the receivers start closer to the attack line.

2. Stress team accomplishments by working in groups of three and rotating when the team achieves a predetermined number of points.

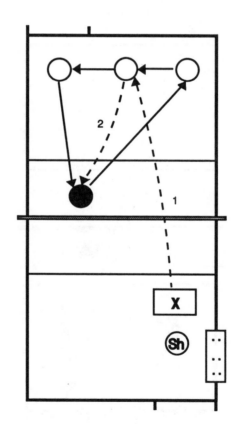

92 RECEIVING REACTION DRILL

Objective: To develop quickness and agility in service reception.

Description: Two players assume positions to receive the serve in the back court; a setter is ready to receive their passes at the net. Additional players line up at the baseline behind the receivers. The coach stands on a table at the opposite baseline and puts the ball in play to one of the receivers (left or right) (1). Upon receiving the serve, the receiver quickly passes to the setter (2) and goes to the end of the line (3). The next player in line moves into the vacant position (4) as the coach then serves to the opposite side, (5) and the drill continues.

Variations:

1. Alter the positions of the receivers.

2. Shorten the reaction time required of the receiver by moving the coach closer to the net.

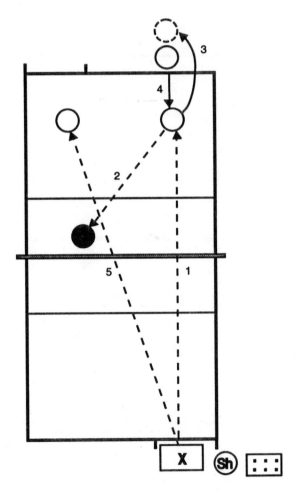

93 GO FOR TWO SERVICE RECEPTION DRILL

Objective: To develop the ability to adjust the angle of the passing platform.

Description: Player A serves to a receiver (B) who is positioned on the left side of the court (1). B passes the ball to the target (2), angling the passing platform. B immediately shuffles to the right (3) while the server is serving a second ball (4). Player B then passes the second ball to the target (5).

Variation: Begin with the receiver on the right side of the court; have the receiver shuffle to the left to pass the second serve.

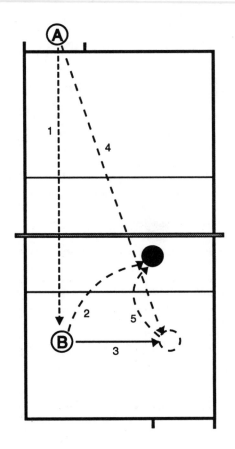

94 COMMUNICATE REACTION DRILL

Objective: To develop verbal and non-verbal communication skills in the service reception.

Description: Two receivers (A and B) are positioned in the middle of the backcourt area, and a target is positioned near the net. The coach serves the ball, and the two receivers must quickly communicate with one another as to who will receive the ball and pass it to the setter, and who will create an "open lane" and assist the teammate receiving the serve.

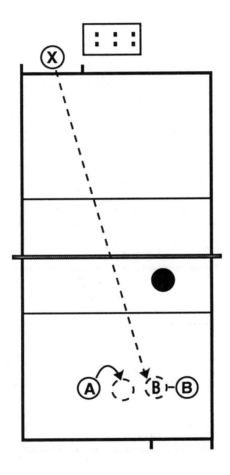

95 TWO-PLAYER SERVICE RECEPTION DRILL

Objective: To develop service reception and team interaction/communication skills.

Description: Two players are positioned in the backcourt to receive the serve. The coach alternates serving to all areas of the court, using a variety of serves. The receivers attempt to pass every ball to the target. While passing, each player should verbally communicate their actions or the movement of the ball (in, out, mine, etc). After a prescribed period of time, or the completion of a set number of serves, the receivers switch positions and the drill continues.

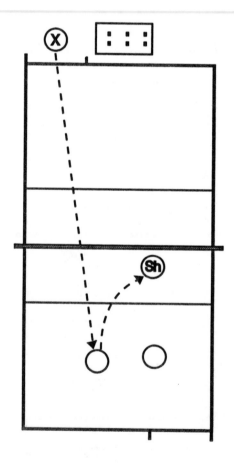

INDIVIDUAL SKILLS

96 DEEP RECEIVING DRILL

Objective: To develop service reception in the two deep positions of a W formation.

Description: A player is positioned backcourt to receive serves. The coach serves the ball alternately to the left and right-back positions of a W service reception formation. The player receiving the serve passes the ball to the target, switches positions and immediately passes again. The same player continues until four consecutive passes are made to the target.

Variations:

1. Vary the direction the receiving player moves.

2. Increase the difficulty of the pass by not serving directly to the receiver.

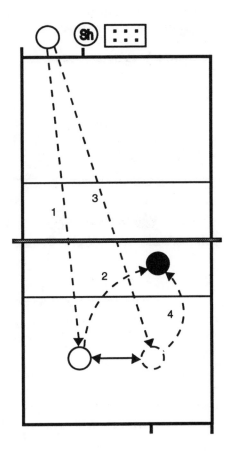

97 SERVE-RECEIVE DRILL

Objective: To develop service reception and serving skills.

Description: Two or three players position themselves in the team's service reception formation, two players are positioned at the net, and the remaining players act as servers as shown in the diagram. A rotating system is used to allow all players to act as servers and receivers. The server puts the ball in play (1). If upon this attempt the ball is successfully passed to a target (2), only the receivers rotate in a clockwise pattern. If the ball fails to reach a target player, the receiver committing the error goes to the serving line and is replaced by the target. The server assumes the vacated spot at the net. Continuous serving should be maintained to develop quickness, agility, and accuracy.

Variations:

1. Alter the receiving formation.

2. Allow the receivers to remain in their positions for an established number of serves, keeping account of passing accuracy. Designate missed serves as good plays for the receivers.

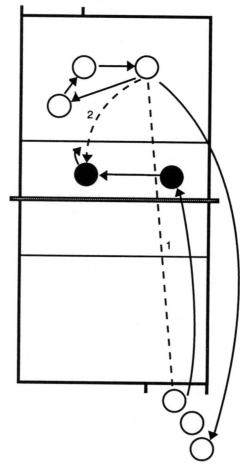

98 ONE-THIRD SERVE AND RECEIVE DRILL

Objective: To develop team service reception and communication skills for one-third of a W formation.

Description: Three players are positioned to form the left side of a W service reception pattern. The coach serves down the line to a receiver (1). The receiver must communicate verbally and with body position as the ball is passed toward the target/setter player (2). The players rotate after a specific number of balls are passed to the target (3).

Variations:

1. Conduct the same drill to either the center or the right third of the W formation.

2. Vary the distance the coach stands from the net.

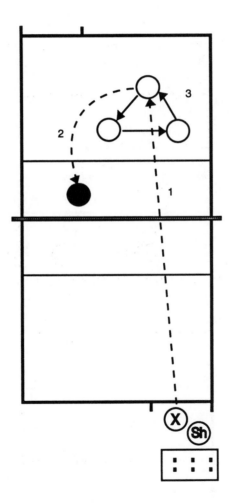

99 SERVE-RECEIVE TRIANGLE DRILL

Objective: To develop passing accuracy and promote communication skills in service reception.

Description: Receivers form a triangular pattern in the center of the court and behind the attack line as shown below. Each server serves a pre-set number of balls to the three receiving positions. The receivers attempt to accurately pass the ball to the setter/target positioned at the net, who catches the ball. Alter receivers' positions in the triangular pattern after a set number of serves. The servers record the number of successful serves. The receivers record the number of successful passes to the target. Following the completion of a pre-set number of service attempts by each server, the servers and receivers switch positions. The group with the highest number of good serves and good passes win.

Variations:

1. Serve directly over the lead player in the triangle.

2. Have the target player set every pass.

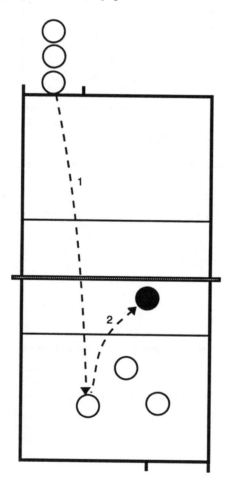

INDIVIDUAL SKILLS

100 TEAM RECEIVE DRILL

Objective: To develop service reception and team coordination skills.

Description: Players are positioned in a W service reception formation. The ball is served randomly to different players and places on the court (1). Receivers concentrate on meeting the ball squarely and making a good pass to a setter/target near the net (2). Players learn to adjust to their teammates, especially when the serve is not hit directly at one player.

Variations:

1. Fewer players can be used to receive the serve.

2. The type, placement, and velocity of the serve can be varied.

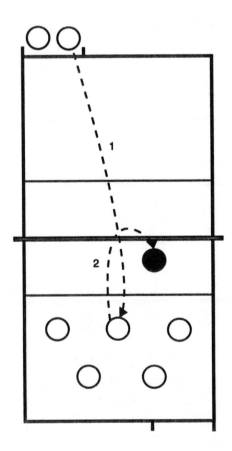

101 SERVE-RECEIVE TO SETTING OPTIONS DRILL

Objective: To develop basic service, reception, and setting skills.

Description: Five players position themselves in a W service reception formation. One player is positioned near the net as a setter. Two more players positioned near the net at each edge of the court serve as targets for the setter as well as shaggers for missed sets. The ball is served to a random receiver (1) who passes the ball to the setter (2). The setter sets to one of the shaggers (3). After two serves, all players rotate clockwise.

Variations:

1. The velocity of the serve can gradually be increased as the drill progresses.

2. The player receiving the serve can be predesignated (as opposed to randomly determined).

3. The server can start serving fifteen feet from the net and gradually move backward.

4. The position of the targets/shaggers should be changed to work on specific sets.

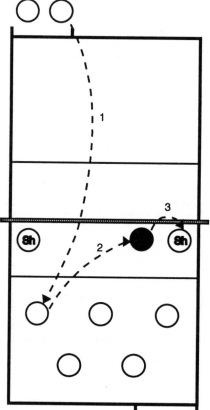

INDIVIDUAL SKILLS

102 TWO OR THREE PLAYER SERVE RECEIVE DRILL

Objective: To develop full team serve receive using a two or three player serve receive system.

Description: Players B and C are the primary passers for a two player serve receive pattern. Player A can be used for short serves or moved back for reception of a jump serve as shown. Player D is a non-passer that supports the team serve receive by call the ball "in" or "out" and supports the passer in case of an emergency. Player E is the quick hitter and will practice various attack options with the setter. Players F, G, and H are the opposing servers who serve various types of serves. Each player will serve and then rotate to the end of the serving line. The next server will wait until the team receives and attacks before serving the next ball.

Variations:

1. Add a block opposing the attack.

2. Utilize the server as a digger after the serve.

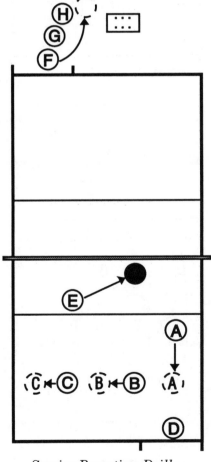

103 BACK ROW ATTACK SERVICE RECEPTION DRILL

Objective: To develop the necessary skills needed to effectively create a backcourt attack in the service reception.

Description: This drill can only be used when both the service reception and back row attack have been mastered. Two players are positioned backcourt to receive the serve, and a setter is positioned near the net. The drill is initiated by the coach serving to either side of the court (1). The receiver closest to the ball will pass to the setter (2) and continue toward one of the three backcourt attack zones, A, B, or C, to spike (3). The setter will set to the appropriate zone (4). The receiver will then spike the ball over the net (5) before going to the end of the receiver line.

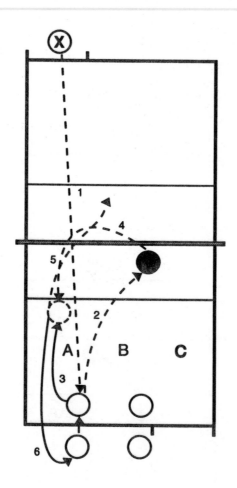

INDIVIDUAL SKILLS

CHAPTER 4

SETTING DRILLS

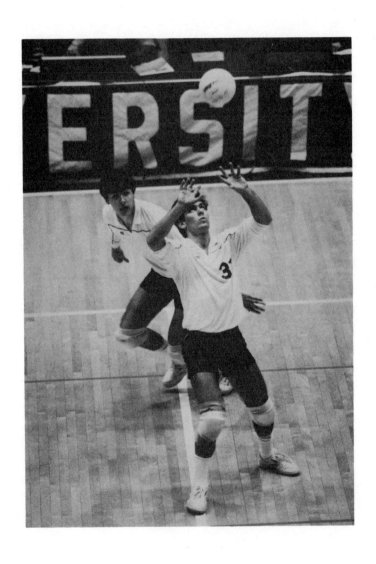

104 OVERHAND PASS DRILL

Objective: To improve execution of overhand pass technique and ball control

Description: Player A passes to B (1), B passes back to A (2), A passes to C (3), and C passes back to A (4).

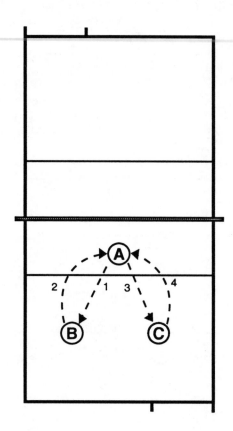

105 CIRCLE PASS DRILL

Objective: To develop passing skills, movement and teamwork.

Description: Split the team into two groups, each forming a circle. One circle will move in a clockwise direction while the other circle will move in a counterclockwise direction. Player A passes the ball to player B (1). As the players' circles continue to rotate, player B passes to C (2). Player C passes to D, and the drill continues.

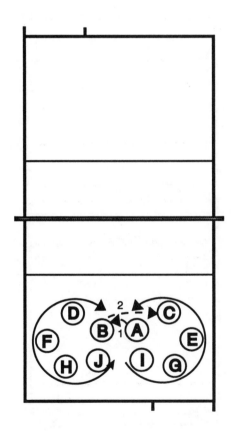

106 FOUR CORNER ZIG-ZAG DRILL

Objective: To develop overhand passing technique.

Description: Players form four single file lines in each corner of the court on the sidelines. Player A in the left-back (#5) position puts the ball in play by setting to B (1) in the right-front (#2) position on the same side. After a set, each player will move to the end of the line as quickly as possible to allow the next player to step into their place on the court. The drill is continued by setting the ball to C located in the left-front (#4) position (2). C sets over to player D in the right-back (#1) position (3). D sets to the new player in the #5 position, beginning the drill sequence again (4).

Variation: Utilize two balls, introducing the second after the first ball has been set diagonally to the #2 position.

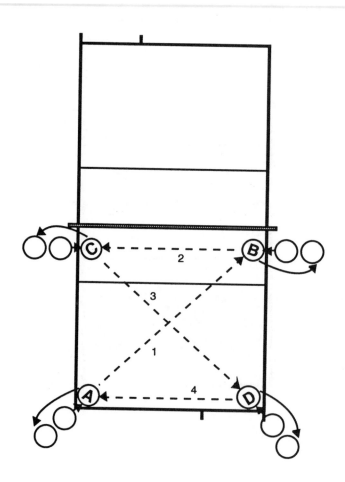

INDIVIDUAL SKILLS

107 CONTINUOUS SETTING DRILL

Objective: To increase the ability to set to different positions at the net. Player A in the center-front (#3) position begins the drill by setting to player B in the (#2) right-front position(1). B sets over A to C, who is in the left-front (#4) position (2). C then sets across the net to D in the #3 position (3). D sets to E on the same side of the net in the #2 position (4), who in turn sets over D to F in the #4 position (5). F then sets across the net to A (6), who will begin the drill sequence again.

Variation: Use two players in each position and have them switch with each other

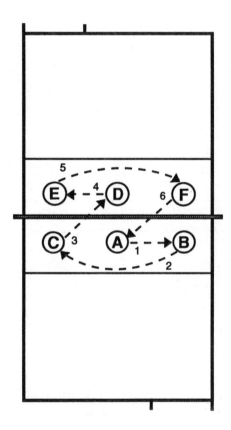

108 BALL CONTROL DRILL

Objective: To improve ability to pass after movement.

Description: Players A and B both have balls which they simultaneously pass to players C and D (1). Immediately after passing, A and B will exchange positions and partners (2). Player C will return pass to A and player D will return pass to B (3). Players A and B will pass back to C and D, respectively, (4) before again exchanging positions to receive the next passes.

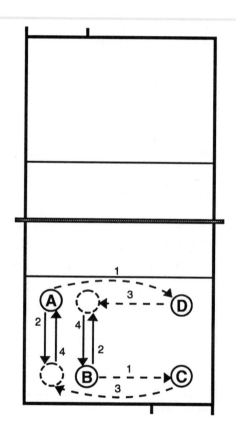

109 STATIONARY AIR SET DRILL

Objective: To develop overhand passing technique and ball control.

Description: The players are lined up parallel to the net. The first player in line sets the ball directly overhead. Immediately after the set, the first player runs to the end of the line. The second player moves under the ball and sets the ball again directly overhead.

Variation: This drill can also be run perpendicular to the net.

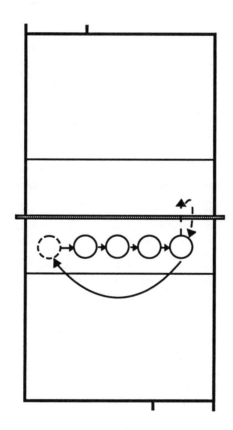

110 BACKSETTING DRILL

Objective: To develop backsetting skills and increase the ability to accurately set from audible clues.

Description: The drill is performed in three-player groups. The first player of the group (A) self-sets the ball three times while walking forward. After the three sets are completed (1,2,3), the next player in line (B) calls out the player's name, signalling the distance (by sound) to backset (4). A then returns to the end of the line.

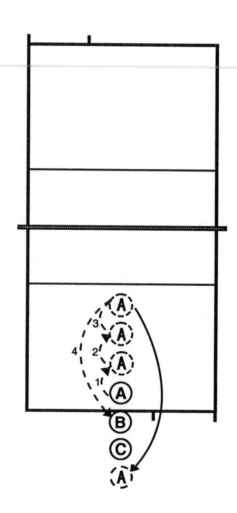

INDIVIDUAL SKILLS

111 RELAY SETTING DRILL

Objective: To develop proper overhand passing technique.

Description: Split the team into equal groups. Have them line up about 3-5 feet apart in two rows on one side of the room and establish a finish line on the opposite side. Players A start the drill by setting the ball to players B (1). After setting the ball, A runs to the front of the line (2). Player B continues the drill by setting to C (3) and also runs to the front of the line. This action continues until one team reaches the finish line.

Variation: Have the players perform the drill in reverse using a back set.

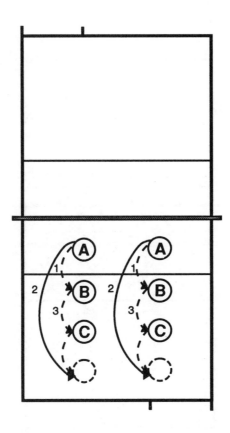

112 QUICK AS A CAT DRILL

Objective: To develop overhead passing skills and player quickness.

Description: Four players line up along the net. Player A starts the drill by self-setting the ball(1), and then setting to player B (2). Player B self-sets (3), turns under the ball and then sets to player C (4). Player C repeats the sequence and sets to player D (5,6). Player D self-sets (7) and then sets the ball the length of the net back to player A (8). After each player sets, they must touch the attack line and then quickly return to pass the next ball.

Variations:

1. Have the players touch the baseline instead of the attack line.

2. Have the players use an emergency technique to approach the attack line.

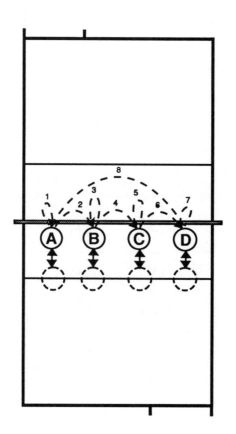

INDIVIDUAL SKILLS

113 SEESAW DRILL

Objective: To improve proper movement and execution of the overhand pass.

Description: Player A sets to player B (1). After the ball is set, player A retreats to the sideline to receive a set ball from player B (2). After setting (3), A immediately returns to the original position to receive a second ball from player B (4). After receiving and returning two balls from player B, player A will set the ball to player B who will move and set (5,6).

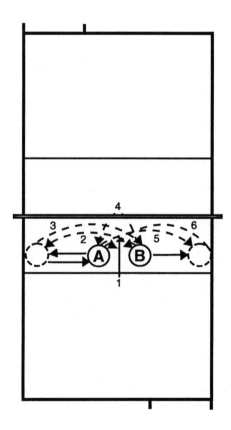

114 FREEBALL SETTING DRILL

Objective: To improve execution of the overhand pass with movement.

Description: Player A initiates this exercise by setting the ball to player B (1). As soon as B return sets the ball (2), A will run to take B's position, and D will step forward into A's place to receive the ball. B will move to take D's former position, and D will set the ball to player C (3). C will set back to B (4) who has stepped up into D's position, and D will run to take C's place.

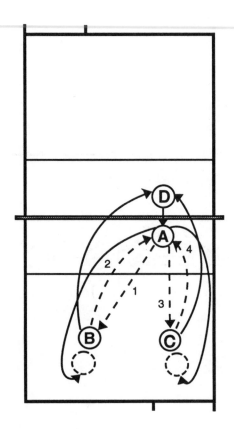

INDIVIDUAL SKILLS

115 BACK COURT SET DRILL

Objective: Develop the skill and accuracy of setting from the backcourt.

Description: Player A tosses a ball deep into the backcourt (1) making player B run to set the ball back to A (2). A practices an approach and jump but catches the ball instead of spiking. Player A goes to the end of the setting line after giving the ball to B, who has gone to the end of the spiking line.

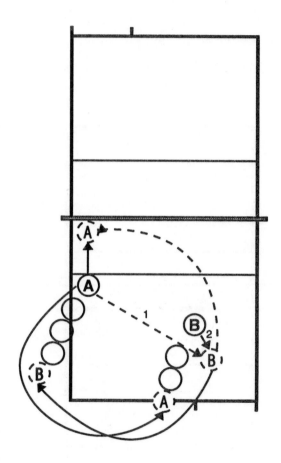

116 NON-STOP BACKCOURT SETTING DRILL

Objective: To develop the skills necessary for backcourt setting and setting along the net.

Description: Player A begins by setting the ball to B in the left-front (#4) position (1). A immediately moves to the back of the line, and B sets the ball to C in the right-front (#2) position (2). C sets the ball to either the right-back (#1) position or the center-back (#6) position (3). The next backcourt player in line continues the drill by moving to the ball and setting to the #4 position.

Variations:

1. The backcourt players can set from the left-back (#5) and center-back (#6) positions to the right-front (#2) position.

2. The first setter can approach the net and jumpset.

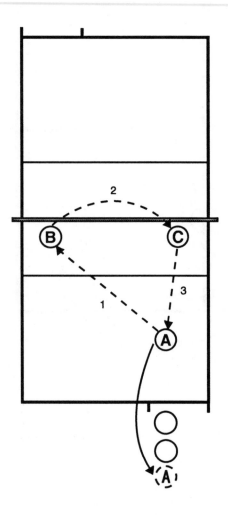

117 SIDE TO SIDE SETTING DRILL

Objective: To develop movement combined with setting and to improve ability to set along the net.

Description: Player A starts the drill by setting the ball to player B in the right-front (#2) position (1). Player B sets back to the left-front (#4) position (2). After setting players go to the end of their respective lines, and the next player in line moves to receive a set. As A moves to the end of the line, C moves into the #4 position to receive B's set. This drill is continuous.

Variation: The drill can also be done with players switching lines after setting to receive sets from both positions.

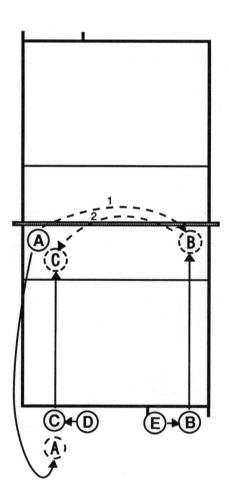

118 JUMPSETTING DRILL

Objective: To develop jumpsetting techniques to a target.

Description: Player A begins the drill by jumpsetting the ball vertically and then sprints to the baseline. Player B runs to the net, jumpsets, and sprints a similar distance. The sequence is then continued by players C and D. The height of the set is determined by the time needed for the next player to get into position.

Variations:

1. Use regular sets instead of jumpsets.

2. Incorporate more players by having multiple stations of the drill.

3. Shorten the distance the players have to sprint.

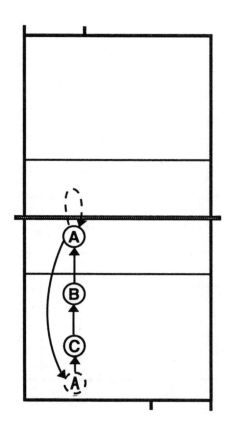

119 SET AND SPRINT DRILL

Objective: Warmup exercise that improve movement and ball control. Conditioning drill.

Description: Four players line up along the net as pictured in the diagram. Player A begins the drill by setting a ball to player C (1), C passes to B (2), B to D (3), and D to A (4), who will continue the drill by again passing to C. After each player passes the ball to the next, the player will run around the baseline and return to original position to receive the next ball.

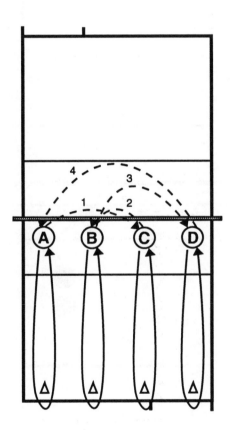

120 TRIANGLE SETTER TRAINING DRILL

Objective: To develop speed and agility of setter.

Description: Player A starts drill by setting to player B (1). The first setter immediately penetrates to the setters zone as B passes the ball to the setter's zone (2). The setter must execute an accurate set to player A (3), and then return to the line. As player A sets to B, the second setter will penetrate and prepare to set.

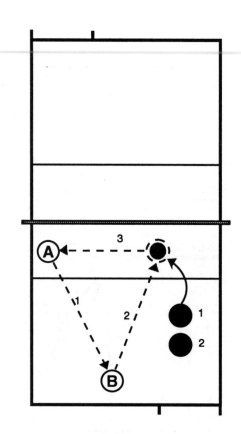

INDIVIDUAL SKILLS

121 DOWN, UP, AND SET DRILL

Objective: To develop accuracy in setting after movement.

Description: Player A puts the ball in play from the left-front (#4) position by setting to player B (1). At the same time, the first setter gets up from a supine position on the floor, and sprints to the setting zone. Player B delivers the ball to the setting zone (2), where the setter must execute an accurate set to player A and then return to the setting line (3). When player A contacts the ball, the second setter gets up from the floor and sprints to the net, and the drill continues.

Variation: Require the setter to use different sets

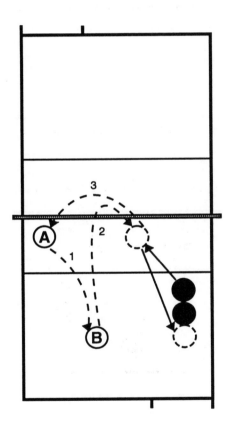

122 CHANGING DIRECTIONS AND SET DRILL

Objective: To develop the setter's ability to change direction while delivering an accurate set. To enhance the setter's ability to disguise the actual set by using a fake technique in setting.

Description: Player A initiates the drill by setting the ball in front of the setter (1). The setter steps forward into the ball and pivots, as if to set the ball to the right-front (#2) position. The setter actually backsets to B in the left-front (#4) position (2). B passes the ball to A to commence the drill again.

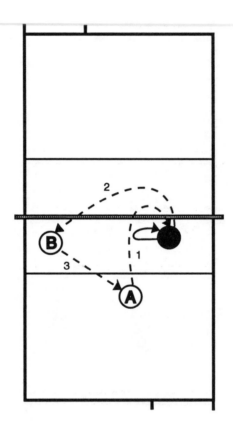

123 THREE PERSON JUMPSET DRILL

Objective: To develop jumpsetting and setting ability close to the net.

Description: Three players line-up the width of the court. Player A is located in the left-front (#4) position and faces player B, located right of center as shown in the diagram. Player C is located in the right-front (#2) position. Player A jumpsets to B (1), B in turn jump-backsets to C (2), who jumpsets the full width of the net back to A (3).

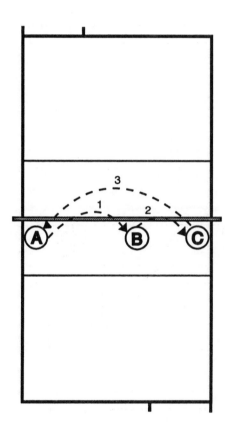

124 ROTATION JUMPSETTING DRILL

Objective: To develop overhand passing control and the skill of jumpsetting.

Description: The drill begins with player A setting to player B (1). After setting, A runs to prepare to assume C's position. Player B jumpsets the ball to player C (2). Immediately after the jumpset, B runs to assume A's former position. C then passes to B and runs to fill B's old position and the drill continues.

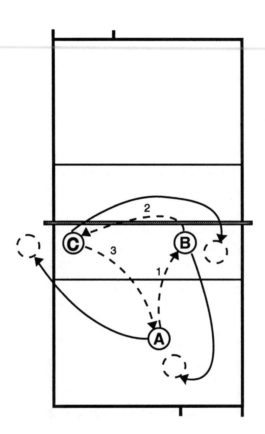

125 JUMPSET AND SPRINT DRILL

Objective: To develop jumpsetting skills in spikers.

Description: Player A in the right-front (#2) position initiates the drill by
setting to player B in the left-front (#4) position (1). Player B jumpsets
back to position #2 (2). Player C steps up to receive the ball and jumpset
it back to player D in position #4 (3). Upon completing the jumpset,
each player sprints to the baseline, returns to the end of the line, and
the drill is continued.

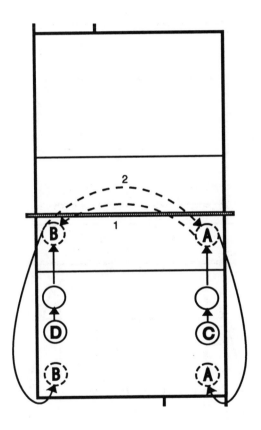

126 THREE PLAYER JUMPSET AND SPRINT DRILL

Objective: To develop jumpsetting skills.

Description: Player A in the right-front (#2) position initiates the drill by setting to player B in the left-front (#4) position (1.) Player B jumpsets to player C (2). Player C jump backsets to the #2 position to player D (3). Player D continues the sequence by jumpsetting to player E in the #4 position. After each player executes a jumpset they go to the end of a new line, moving in a counter clockwise order.

Variation: Have player B in the left-front (#4) position begin the drill by jumpsetting to player C. C jumpsets back to B who will jumpset full-court to player A. A returns the full-court jumpset to player E in the #4 position who continues the drill.

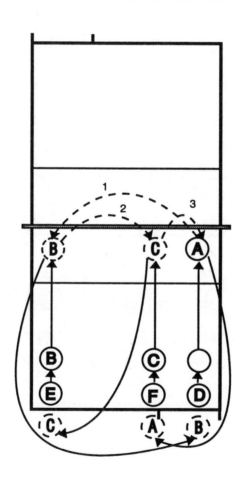

INDIVIDUAL SKILLS

127 SEMI-CIRCULAR SETTING DRILL

Objective: To develop proper setting technique.

Description: The coach puts the ball in play by tossing it directly above the head of the first player in line (1). Upon contact with the ball, the player utilizes an overhand pass to hit the ball to the shagger in the left-front (#4) position (2). This player then moves to the end of the line (3).

Variations:

1. The ball can be set to the right-front (#2) position.

2. The ball may be bounced high to force the player to move under it before setting it.

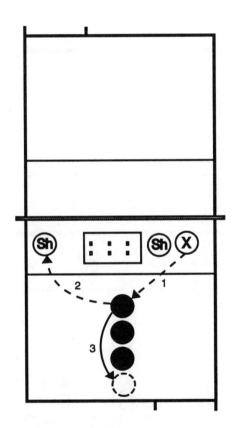

128 RAPID FIRE FREEBALL DRILL

Objective: To develop overhead setting techniques to be used for freeball passes.

Description: The coach puts the ball in play by tossing it to mid-court. Player A moves towards the net from the baseline and sets to the target (1). While player A is setting, the coach tosses another ball mid-court to player B, who also sets towards the target (2). A third ball is then tossed by the coach which activates player C (3). After setting, all players return to the baseline and get ready to re-initiate the drill sequence.

Variations:

1. Toss the ball at a variety of heights.

2. Require the players to touch the wall instead of the baseline to increase conditioning.

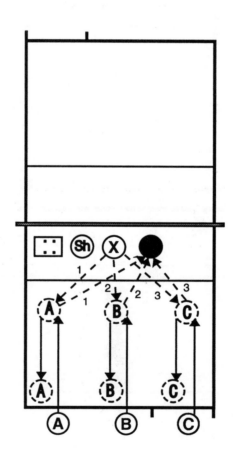

129 BREAD AND BUTTER DRILL

Objective: To promote the skill of backcourt setting.

Description: The coach tosses the ball deep into the left-back (#5) position (1). Player A sprints into position behind the ball and sets a high ball to the right-front (#2) position (2). The coach tosses a ball deep to the right-back (#1) position (3). Player A sprints into position behind the ball and sets it high to the left-front (#4) position (4). A returns to the end of the line, allowing another to execute the same movements.

Variation: The coach can initiate the drill from different positions on the same side of the net or from the opposite side of the net.

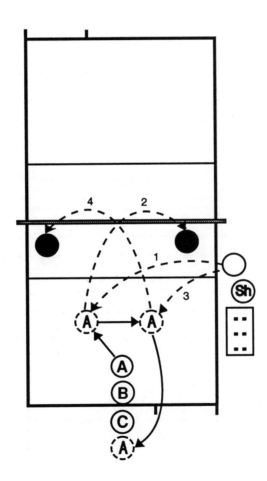

130 RUN IT DOWN DRILL

Objective: To teach team interaction in running down a ball going out of play.

Description: The coach puts the ball in play by spiking it off the hand, similar to a blocker touching a ball, outside the court (1). The spike signals the two defensive players to turn and move rapidly toward the ball. The player closest to the ball calls "mine" and passes the ball to the trailing player (2). The trailing player sets to either target (3).

Variations:

1. Conduct the drill from the right and center-back defensive positions.

2. Require the targets to spike the ball.

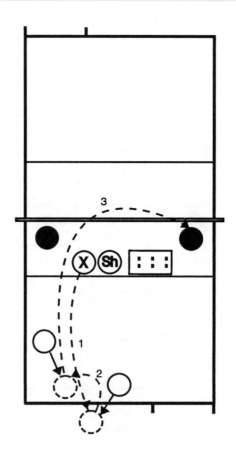

INDIVIDUAL SKILLS

131   FREEBALL & SET DRILL

Objective: To develop simple setting and freeball passing skills.

Description: The coach initiates the drill by tossing a ball to any of the three players lined-up across the court (1). The player tossed the ball has to overhand pass it to the setter (2). The setter sets to a prescribed target or basket along the net (3). After each freeball pass, the player passing the ball is replaced by an on deck player.

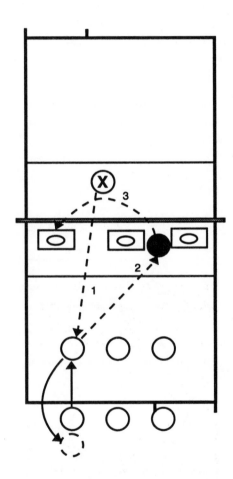

132 SETTING ACCURACY AND MOVEMENT DRILL

Objective: To develop backcourt setting.

Description: The coach sets the ball to the right-back (#1) position (1). Player A moves from the center-back (#6) position, runs around a cone in the #1 position, and sets to player B in the left-front (#4) position (2). B immediately passes back to the coach (3), who sets the ball deep into the #4 position. A runs around the second cone located near the #4 position and sets to B (5), who has moved to the right-front (#2) position. B jumpsets to the coach (6) while A assumes B's spot at the #4 position. B moves to the end of the backcourt setting line. C moves into A's starting position, and the drill is repeated.

Variation: Run the drill to the opposite side.

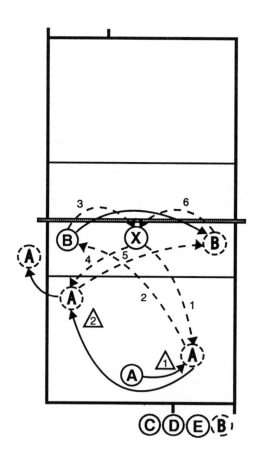

133 WEAVE AND SET DRILL

Objective: To develop accuracy and setting ability after movement.

Description: Three players form a single-file line parallel to the sideline near the net. The coach is positioned on the opposite side of the net at mid-court. Two shaggers are positioned at a 45-degree angle to the coach. The ball is put into play by the coach with a high toss (1). Player A runs under the net (2) and sets the ball to the shagger on the far sideline (3). As A runs under the net on the far opposite side (4), a second ball is tossed, (5) and player A repeats the above steps and sets the ball to the shagger closest to the original starting point (6). A then returns to the end of the line (7). Every succeeding player in the line is required to perform the same setting skill, after crossing under the net.

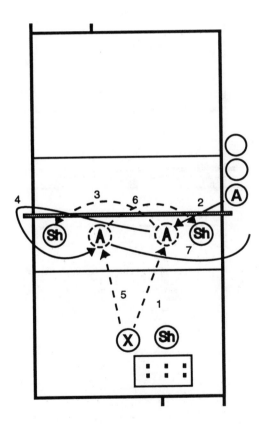

134 SETTER DECISION DRILL

Objective: To develop the awareness and peripheral vision of the setter.

Description: The coach tosses a ball to the setter. When the setter is about to receive the ball, the blocker makes a move to one side or the other. The setter should watch by peripheral vision which way the blocker moves and set in the opposite direction to one of the shaggers.

Variation: Use a small blocker and a tall blocker. The setter needs to set in the direction the small blocker goes.

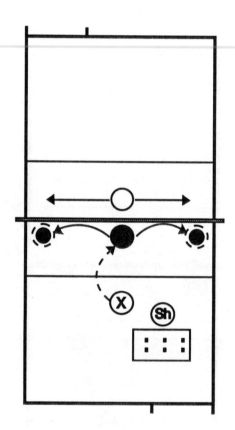

INDIVIDUAL SKILLS

135 AUDIBLE SETTING DRILL

Objective: To train the setter to make a particular set off of an audible call during play.

Description: The coach tosses the ball to the net. The setter runs in from the 10-foot line and the coach yells out a type of set to be executed. The setter then sets to one of the players at the net. For example, if, when the ball is tossed and the setter runs in, the coach yells "back," the setter would execute a back set.

Variation: To increase the difficulty of the drill, have the player execute a jumpset each time.

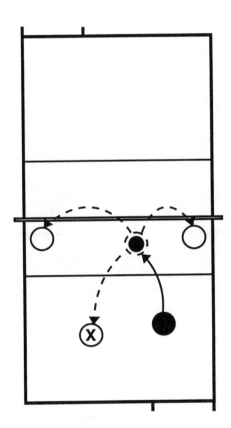

136 SPRINT-TO-SET DRILL

Objective: To develop the setter's range and foot speed.

Description: The coach slaps the ball, signalling A to begin sprinting. The ball is put into play with a high toss over the net to the attack line (1). A runs behind and under the ball, setting the ball high, three feet from the sideline to a shagger located at the left-front (#4) position (2).

Variations:

1. Add a spiker to hit the set to make the drill more difficult.

2. Execute the drill with the setter passing the ball to the right-front (#2) position.

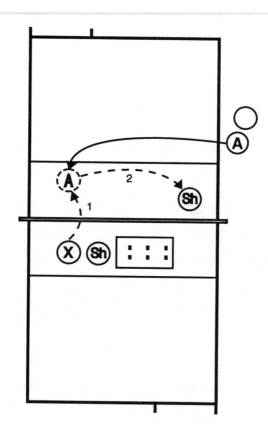

137 SETTER TRANSITION DRILL

Objective: To develop the setter's ability to get into position to run offense after blocking in any position on the net.

Description: The setter starts in the left-front (#4) position. After a mock block the setter sprints to the target area where the coach is tossing the first ball (1). After the setter sets to the #4 position (2) the coach tosses a second ball between 5' to 10' from the net (3). The setter squares up under the ball and again sets to position #4 (4). The setter then leaves the court to be replaced by the next setter in line.

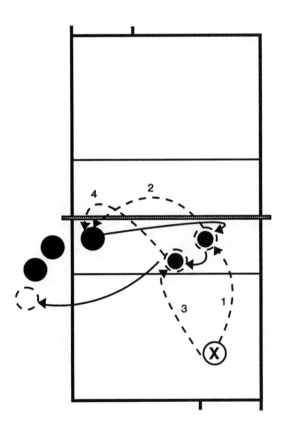

138 FORWARD DRILL

Objective: To develop accuracy and consistency in setting after moving forward and backward.

Description: The coach slaps the ball, signalling the setter to penetrate to the setting area. As the setter is moving toward the net, the coach tosses the first ball (1). The setter sets the ball to the left-front (#4) position (2). Then the coach tosses a ball in front of the setter that requires forward movement before setting to the same position(3). After setting (4), the setter returns to the end of the line in the original setting area, and a third ball is tossed to the next player.

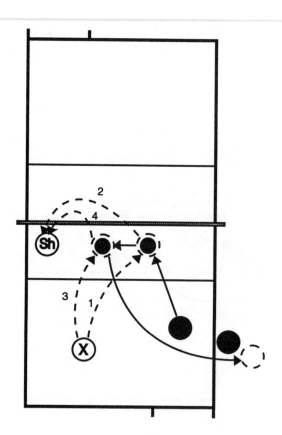

139 SQUARING UP DRILL

Objective: To train the setter to move behind the ball and face the direction and target to which the ball is to be set.

Description: The coach slaps the ball and a setter penetrates to the setters area. As the setter is penetrating, the coach tosses the first ball near the net (1). The setter sets the ball to the left-front (#4) position (2). Then the coach tosses the second ball 8-10 feet from the net (3), forcing the setter to square up and again set to the #4 position (4).

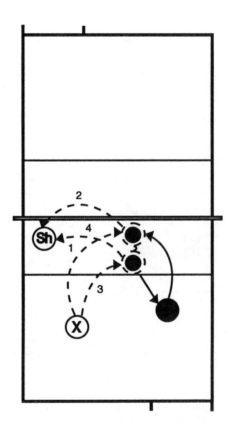

140 SET THREE DRILL

Objective: To develop the setters ability to move forward and backpeddle to reach the ball.

Description: The coach initiates this drill by tossing a ball to the setter's area (1) as the setter is moving down from the right-back position (#1). The setter sets the ball to the left- front (#4) position (2). Then the coach tosses the second ball 6-8 feet from the net and behind the setter (3), forcing the setter to backpeddle and get into position to set the ball to the #4 position (4). The third toss should be forward of the setters area and closer to the net (5). Once the setter has correctly moved into position, the setter should execute a back set to the right-front (#2) position (6).

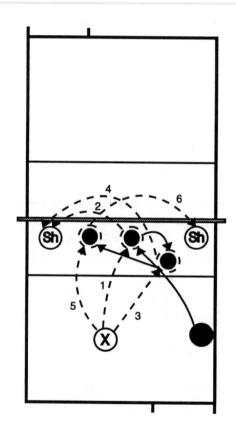

141 LEFT-SIDE PENETRATION DRILL

Objective: To develop efficient and effective penetration from the left-back position.

Description: The setter begins in the left-back (#5) position. The setter penetrates from behind a cone to the setters area at the net as the coach tosses a ball to the setters area (1, 2), putting pressure on the setter to move efficiently into the proper position and deliver an effective set to the left-front (#4) position (2).

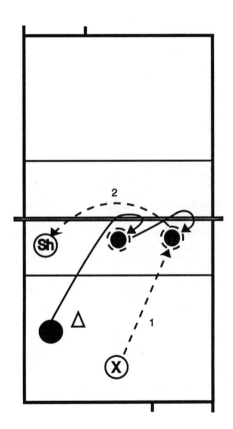

142 BACKPEDDLE & SET DRILL

Objective: To develop movement skills and improve footwork. To develop setting accuracy after employing backward movement.

Description: The setter penetrates from the left-back (#5) position to the setting area at the net. At approximately the same time the setter arrives at the setting area, the coach tosses a ball behind the setter to force backward movement (1). The setter must position correctly to deliver an accurate set to the left-front (#4) position (2).

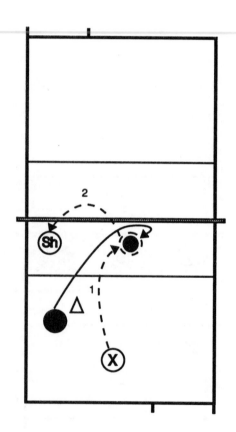

INDIVIDUAL SKILLS

143 SETTER MOVEMENT DRILL

Objective: To increase the movement abilities of the setter in a multiple offense system with emphasis on accuracy, consistency, and endurance.

Description: The coach initiates movement by tossing a ball between the right-front (#2) and the center-front (#3) positions. The setter starts in the right-back (#1) position and runs around an obstacle (chair, cone, etc.) to the target area and sets to the players in either the (#4) left-front, #3, or #2 positions. At that point, the setter runs around an obstacle at the left- back (#5) position. The coach then introduces another ball requiring the setter to set to one of the hitting positions.

Variation: Vary the height of sets, according to the team's offensive system.

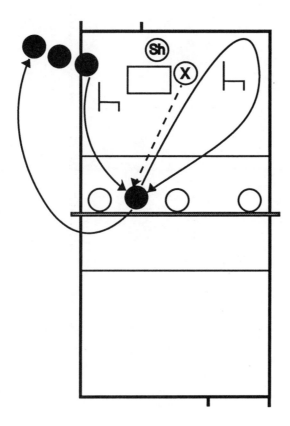

INDIVIDUAL SKILLS

CHAPTER 5

SPIKING DRILLS

144 PROGRESSIVE APPROACH TO HITTING DRILL

Objective: To develop the proper footwork involved in spiking the ball.

Description: The coach diagrams proper foot placement and sequencing on the court with tape, paying attention to the stride lengths of the athletes executing the drill. Each floor marking is designed to increase the stride length and the required speed of movement by the player. The first hitter approaches the net, following the floor markings which diagram the necessary footwork for approaching to spike, and jumps. The player lands, then goes to the end of the next line.

Variation: Have the hitter spike a ball held by someone at the net who is standing on a chair, holding the ball above the net.

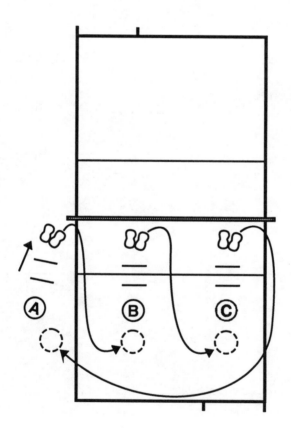

145 PARTNER SPIKING DRILL

Objective: To develop proper body positioning for the up-and- over arm swing used in spiking.

Description: Working in pairs, two hitters assume a position opposite from one another in each court, approximately 15-20 feet from the net. Hitter A self tosses the ball overhead, executes an up-and- over arm swing, and spikes the ball over the net to B. B then repeats the process, while emphasizing proper arm swing and spikes the ball back across the net.

Variations:

1. The hitter bounces the ball directly in front of the hitting shoulder, jumps, and spikes the ball across the net.

2. Have the hitter toss the ball out in front of the hitting shoulder, approach, jump, and spike the ball.

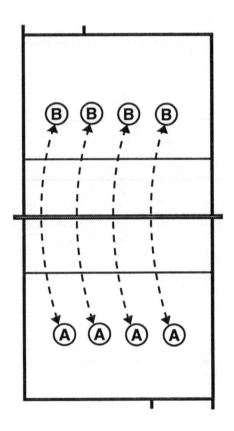

146 JUST SPIKE-IT DRILL

Objective: To develop the techniques for a proper approach and spike, with an emphasis on arm extension and ball contact.

Description: Place a "Spike-It" portable device, which suspends a volleyball above the net, at the left front (#4) position. Three hitters form a single line approximately 10 feet from the net. Upon a signal from the coach, each player approaches, jumps and contacts the suspended ball, attempting to use correct spiking form (1). Players then return to the end of the line and continue this process (2).

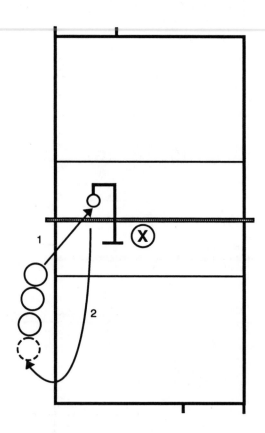

147 SELF-BOUNCE AND SPIKE DRILL

Objective: To teach players how to properly approach and spike, with a special emphasis on opening up the hitting shoulders and correctly positioning their bodies in relation to the ball.

Description: The hitters bounce the ball on the floor in front of their bodies with sufficient force to propel it above their heads (1). Each player moves to the ball (2) using proper approach steps. The player then spikes the ball across the net to the shaggers (3).

Variations:

1. Have the players vary the direction that they bounce the ball.

2. Have the spikers hit the ball to a specific area on the court.

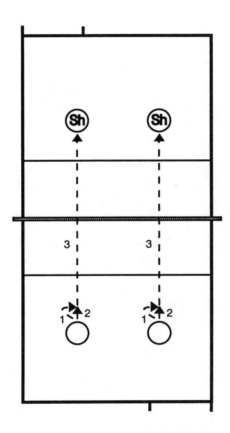

148 SPIKE THE BOUNCE DRILL

Objective: To develop the techniques for approaching and the correct positioning for spiking.

Description: The hitters form a single-file line (middle-deep) on the court as illustrated below. The drill is initiated when the coach is handed a ball by the shagger. The coach bounces the ball to the first hitter who approaches the bounced ball using proper positioning (1) and spikes the ball. After spiking, the spiker retrieves the ball and returns to the line (2).

Variations:

1. Have the hitter spike the ball to a specific area of the court.

2. Have the coach vary the location of where the ball is bounced.

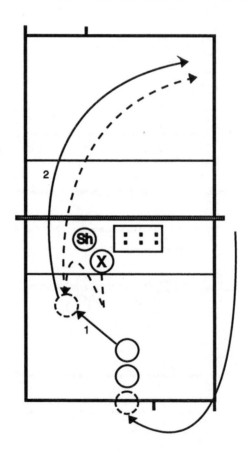

INDIVIDUAL SKILLS

149 QUICK TOSS DRILL

Objective: To develop the approach and arm swing for the quick middle hit.

Description: The players line up at a 30 degree angle off the perpendicular from the net. The coach, positioned next to the net on the same side of the court, puts a ball in play for each hitter. Each player come to the net while performing the proper approach and arm swing. The coach tosses the ball directly into the spiker's hand as the spiker's arm is swinging forward. After spiking, the player returns to the end of the line and a new player steps up to the coach.

Variations:

1. Vary the position from which the coach tosses the ball.

2. Toss the ball to an attacking spiker for a 31 or half-shoot.

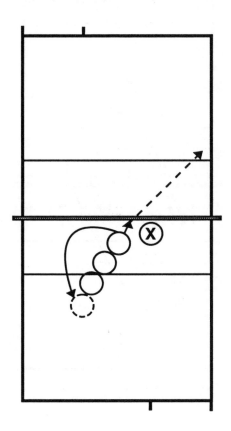

150 RAPID FIRE SPIKING

Objective: Develop spiking technique and get maximum number of contacts.

Description: The coach tosses the ball to hitter A (1) who approaches (2) and spikes the ball over the net (3). Player A shags the ball and returns it to the coach, then goes to the end of the line (4).

Variations:

1. Toss from different locations at the net

2. Vary the height of the tosses.

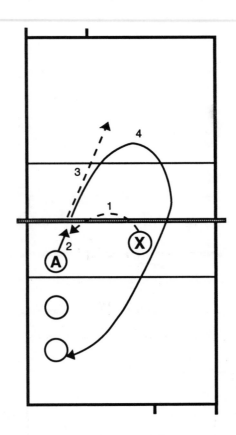

INDIVIDUAL SKILLS

151 ENDURANCE HITTING DRILL

Objective: To develop hitting endurance with an emphasis on timing and proper approach.

Description: Three players form a single line at the 10 foot line. The coach tosses the ball (1) to player A who approaches and spikes the ball (2). Immediately, the coach tosses a second ball for player B to spike. Upon the completion of player A's spike, A runs around a chair located on the endline. At this time the coach is already beginning to toss the third ball to player C. Player A rounds the chair (3) and becomes the next player appraching for the ball.

Variations:

1. Require the spiker to accurately hit the ball to a marked spot.

2. Change the types of and the positions from where the toss is made.

3. Add blockers to increase the complexity and the difficulty of the drill.

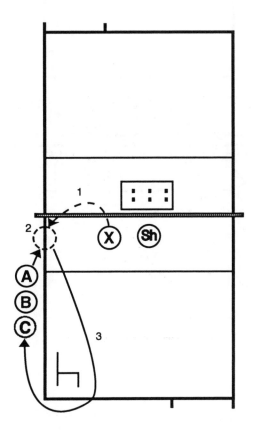

152 MULTI-POSITION HITTING DRILL

Objective: To develop spiking skills under pressure and to provide over-all conditioning.

Description: Player B feeds a ball to the left-front (#4) position (1). Player A spikes the ball and immediately runs around an obstacle (2) readying for the next ball which is delivered by C to the center-front position (3). Player A spikes again, then runs around a second obstacle (4) to receive a ball from D in the right-front (#2) position (5). Upon completion of the third spike, A immediately returns to the left side of the court (6) and continues the circuit.

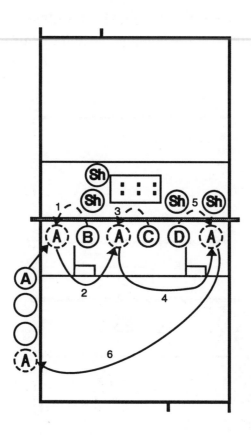

INDIVIDUAL SKILLS

153 V.S.T. (VARIABLE SPEED AND TRAJECTORY) DRILL

Objective: To teach players to spike balls delivered to them at various speeds and trajectories and from various positions.

Description: The coach assumes a position away from the net and behind the attackline. Each group consists of three hitters who are positioned as shown in the diagram. The coach tosses the ball to the left-front (#4) position, utilizing a variety of speeds and trajectories (1). The hitters must adjust the length and speed of their approach to establish positioning for a successful spike (2). After each spike, the player will move to the end of the line (3).

Variations:

1. Have the players execute the same drill at the right-front (#2) position.

2. Change the position from which the coach tosses the ball.

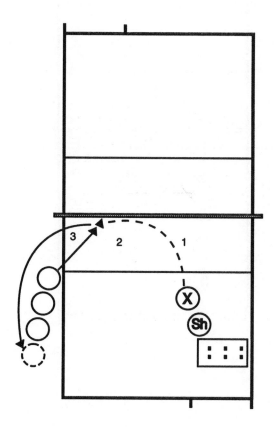

154 THE TIPPER DRILL

Objective: To teach players how to tip correctly.

Description: The coach tosses the ball for player A near the net. A jumps and tips the ball over B's hands (1). Player B then shags the ball and goes to the end of the spiking line (2).

Variation: Have the Blocker B work on landing and dropping off the net to play the tip.

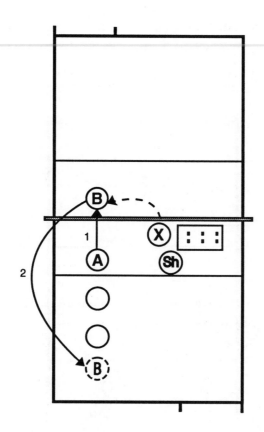

155 BACK ROW ATTACK DRILL

Objective: To develop ability to effectively spike from the back court.

Description: The coach tosses balls at varying distances from the net, between approximately 5 and 10 feet depending upon the ability of the player (1). Player A must jump horizontally and vertically from behind the attack line toward the net, keeping the ball well in front of the body, and spike (2). After spiking, player A shags the ball and returns it to the coach. Player A then returns to the line and the next player will prepare to spike.

Variation: Have the players execute the same drill from the center and the right side of the court.

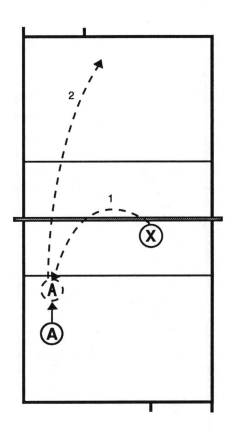

156 DOUBLE BACKCOURT DRILL

Objective: To develop the ability to spike the ball from behind the attack line.

Description: Two players are positioned in the backcourt as shown below. The coach, located in the left-front (#4) position, tosses the ball approximately 2-3 feet in front of the attack line to the left-back (#5) position player, A. Player A approaches (1), jumps behind the attack line, and spikes the ball to the #5 position on the opposite court. Player A then shags the ball (2), returns it to the coach (3), and goes to the end of the line in the right-back (#1) position (4). Another coach tosses a ball in the same fashion to the #1 position player, B. Player B then executes the same movements to spike the ball to the #1 position on the opposite court.

Variations:

1. Have the players hit the ball to a variety of positions on the opposite side of the net.

2. Have the players hit the ball from a variety of positions.

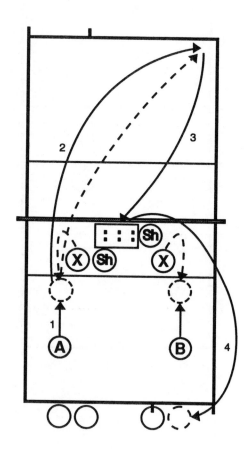

157 CROSS-COURT SPIKING DRILL

Objective: To develop the ability to hit cross-court with the presence of a cross-court blocker.

Description: The coach tosses or sets the ball to player A (1), who will spike the ball cross-court to C (2). B positions to block line, forcing A to spike cross-court. C either self- bumps or shags the ball, returns it to the coach (3), and goes to the end of the spiking line (4). A steps into B's former position (5), and B moves to take C's place (6).

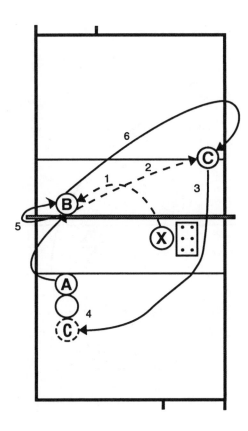

158 SPIKE LINE DRILL

Objective: To develop ability to spike along the sideline with the presence of a cross-court blocker.

Description: The coach tosses the ball to the setter (1) who sets the ball to player A (2). Player A spikes the ball to C (3). Player B blocks cross-court forcing A to spike along the sideline. C self-digs the ball (4) and then returns the ball to the coach. A moves to assume B's postition, B moves to take C's position, and C goes to the end of the spiking line.

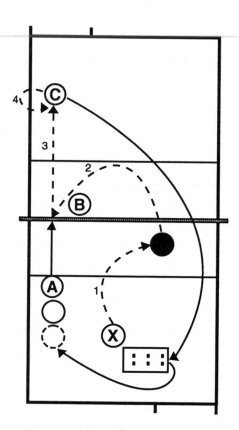

INDIVIDUAL SKILLS

159 TARGET HITTING

Objective: To develop ability to hit high and deep to the right-back (#1) and left-back (#5) positions.

Description: Two mats are placed on the floor across the net in the #1 and #5 positions. The spiker, A, passes the ball to the setter (1), who in turn sets the ball to A in the left-front (#4) position (2). Player A spikes the ball to either of the two mats (3).

Variations:

1. Have the players spike from the middle-front (#3) position or the right-front (#2) position.

2. Add a blocker to take one of the two shots away.

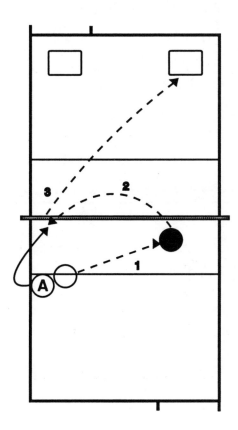

160 COMMAND SPIKING DRILL

Objective: To develop the ability to spike to specific areas on command.

Description: Three mats are placed on the floor and numbered as shown below. Player A tosses the ball to the setter (1) who sets the ball back to A (2). As A leaves the floor to spike, the coach calls out a number designating the area the player is to spike the ball (3). Player A retrieves the ball and goes to the end of the spiking line (4).

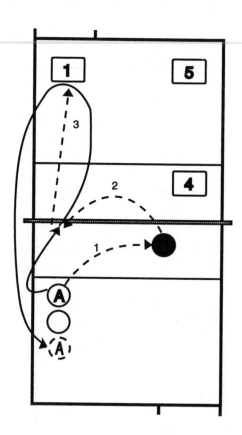

161 TRANSITION SPIKING DRILL

Objective: To develop endurance and improve quickness of transition.

Description: The coach begins the drill by tossing the ball to the setter (1). The setter sets to player A (2) who spikes (3) and immediately returns to starting position (4). As A is moving, another ball is tossed to the setter and set to A. Player A approaches and spikes a second ball, then returns again to receive a third set. The shaggers must hustle to insure that the coach does not run out of balls. This drill is to be a high intensity stressful drill.

Variations:

1. Have A hit from all positions.

2. Have the coach toss balls to the setter just before A has hit the set to force A to make the transition more quickly.

3. Have the coach toss balls at a variety of speeds and require the hitter to adjust the transition accordingly.

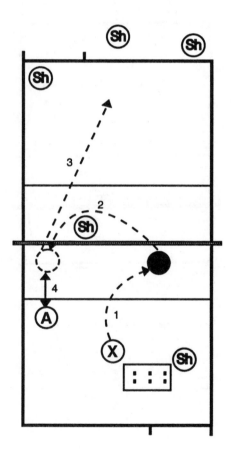

162 QUICK ATTACK DRILL

Objective: To develop the correct technique and timing for the quick attack.

Description: The coach initiates the drill from the left-back (#5) position by tossing to the setter at the net (1). Player A, while watching the trajectory of the toss to help determine the approach angle and timing, follows the toss to the setter (2). As the toss is descending on the setter, A begins to jump . A should be a hand-shake's distance from the setter at take-off, and be in the air at the moment the setter sets the ball (3). Player A then spikes and shags the ball returning it to the coach (4).

Variations:

1. Change the position of the coach tossing the ball.

2. Vary the trajectory and speed of the tosses.

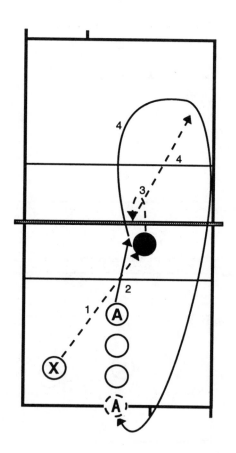

INDIVIDUAL SKILLS

163 PLAY SET DEVELOPMENT DRILL

Objective: To develop the abilities of both the quick hitter and the playset hitter.

Description: The coach tosses the ball to the setter. The setter sets to either player A or player B. The player that spikes, shags the ball, the non-hitting player and the spiker then return to the end of the line and two new players step-up.

Variations:

1. Different playsets can be practiced.

2. The position of the coach tossing could be varied.

3. The trajectory and speed of the toss could be varied as well as the distance from the net.

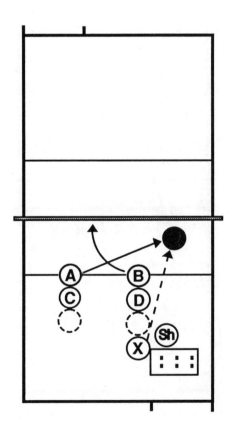

164 ROTATION SPIKING DRILL

Objective: To warm-up spikers before a game. This is also a good drill for teaching basic mechanics of spiking.

Description: Player A tosses the ball to player B (1). Player B sets to C (2), who spikes the ball over the net (3). C retrieves the ball (4) and all players rotate to their left (5), (A goes to line B, B to C, C to A) and the drill continues.

Variations:

1. Run the same drill from all positions.

2. Add a player D as a blocker, and have D shag the spike after the block.

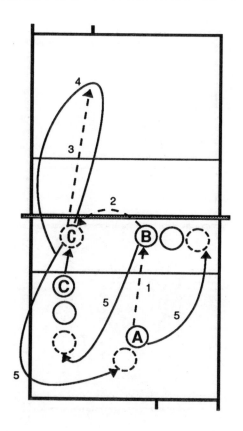

165 TWO-LINE SPIKING DRILL

Objective: To warm-up before a game.

Description: Player A starts the drill by tossing to the setter. The setter alternates setting between lines B and C. The spiker calls for the type of set desired as A tosses the ball to the setter. After spiking, the player shags the ball and goes to the end of the A line to become a tosser. After tossing, the A player goes to the hitting line that the player has not yet visited.

Variations:

1. Add a player D as a blocker opposite the hitting line.

2. Use two setters. Have one set forward and one backset.

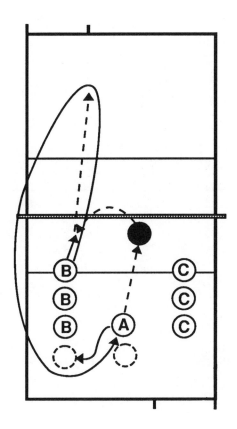

INDIVIDUAL SKILLS

CHAPTER 6

BLOCKING DRILLS

166 WARM-UP BLOCKING DRILL

Objective: To develop body control at the net. To allow the body to warm-up prior to high-intensity work.

Description: Four players assume positions at the net with a ball. Four other players start at the baseline on the other side of the net. The coach signals the players to begin moving. The players at the net jump and toss the ball in a simulated blocking action to the players at the baseline (1). The ball is held overhead with two hands by the tossing players, contracting their abdominal muscles to snap their bodies forward and propel the ball to their partners. After tossing, the players immediately backpedal towards the baseline while their partners are advancing to the net (2).

Variation: Have the tossing players bounce the ball to their partners on the baseline.

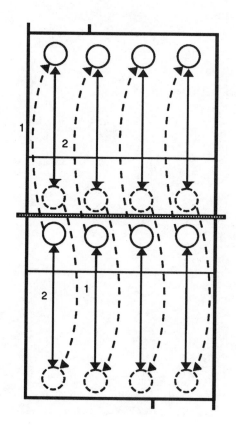

INDIVIDUAL SKILLS

167 CONTINUOUS BLOCKING DRILL

Objective: To develop the footwork and technique involved in blocking.

Description: Six players line up across the court in the blocking positions, with the remainder of the players split into two lines on the right and left sides of the court as illustrated below. Each player begins the drill by jumping and blocking in place. Upon impact with the floor, all players move one blocking position to the right. Players should try to synchronize their blocks with the players opposite them. When blockers steps off the court, they move to come back on the other side of the net.

Variations:

1. Have the players stagger themselves so that they do not face another blocker.

2. Have the players perform the drill moving to the left.

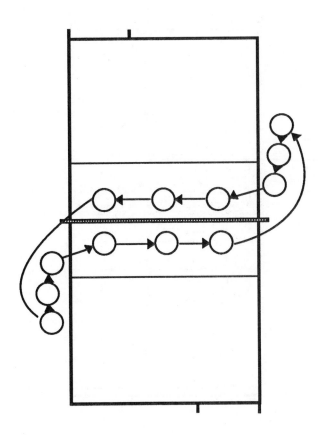

168 FANCY FOOTWORK BLOCKING

Objective: To develop the proper footwork using the shuffle, step-crossover-hop, or step-hop methods.

Description: The blockers assume positions on both sides of the net. With each line beginning at different times, the first blocker in line starts the drill by executing a standing block. Upon contact with the floor, the player executes the shuffle or step-crossover-hop footwork covering approximately 10 feet and blocks. The player then moves in the opposite direction performing a step-hop block. This sequence is repeated until the blocker reaches the opposite side of the court.

Variation: Incorporate a two-player block in the drill.

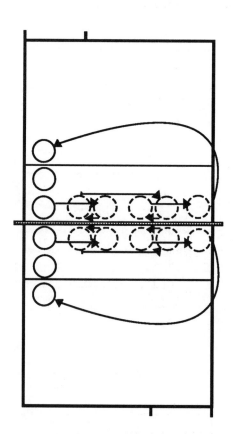

169 RAPID FIRE SIMULATED BLOCKING DRILL

Objective: To develop the proper techniques for form, footwork, and timing involved in blocking.

Description: Five players with balls assume positions approximately eight feet from the net (A). The blockers (B) take turns moving left along the net. The blockers must jump and block each ball the tosser throws just above the top of the net. An emphasis is to be placed on using correct form, footwork, and timing in the block. Shaggers collect the blocked balls and toss them to the tossers as needed.

Variations:

1. Have the blockers move to the right along the net.

2. Have the tossers vary where they toss the ball by tossing a little to the right or left.

3. Have the tossers toss to themselves so they can actually spike at the blockers.

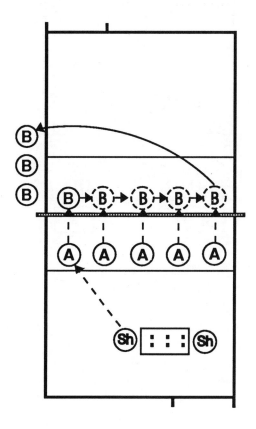

170 SPIKER AWARENESS DRILL

Objective: To develop the blocker's awareness of the opposing spiker's movements and to teach proper blocking techniques.

Description: A blocker assumes a position on the opposite side of the net from the coach. A tosser stands behind the blocker. The tosser (A) initiates the drill by tossing the ball to the coach, who spikes it towards the blocker, B. B watches the movements of the coach to anticipate what must be done to block the ball. After blocking, B shags the ball, and the next player steps onto the court.

Variations:

1. Have the tosser alternate the trajectory of the ball to the coach from right to left to force the blocker to adjust to spikes from a variety of directions.

2. Incorporate two blockers in the drill.

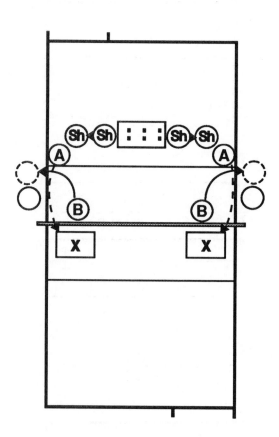

INDIVIDUAL SKILLS

171 CHAIR BLOCKING DRILL

Objective: To develop the proper form and footwork for blocking.

Description: Five players stand on chairs on one side of the net. Each player holds a ball above the net. The blockers move along the other side of the net, with an emphasis on correct footwork, jumping and penetrating to the net to push each ball down in a simulated block. A player returns to the end of the line after contacting all five balls.

Variations:

1. Have the players perform the drill moving left along the net.

2. Have the players on the chairs move the ball from one side to the other to force the blockers to react to movement.

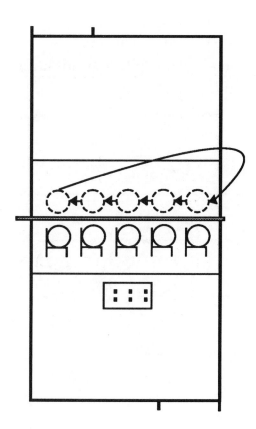

172 TEAM CHAIR BLOCKING DRILL

Objective: To develop the footwork of the middle blocker and to improve techniques for a two-player block.

Description: Three players stand on chairs on one side of the net, each holding a ball above the net. The middle blocker moves to the left, utilizing the correct footwork, and assumes a position next to the outside blocker to form a two-player block (1). This two-person unit jumps and blocks while attempting to penetrate the net and push the ball down in a simulated block. The middle blocker then moves to the right (2), again using the correct footwork, and assumes a position next to the opposite outside blocker to form another two-player blocking team. They repeat the simulated block. When this phase of the drill is completed, the players move to the end of the line (3).

Variations:

1. Have the players perform the drill moving to the right side first.

2. Have the players on the chair move the ball from side to side to make the blockers react to the movement.

3. Have the players on the chair spike the ball instead of just holding it.

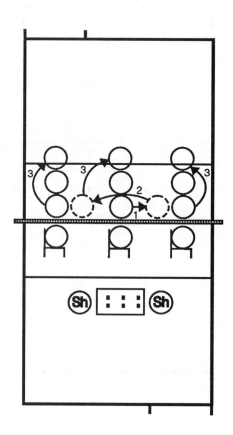

INDIVIDUAL SKILLS

173 NON-STOP BLOCKING DRILL

Objective: To enhance the ability to move laterally and improve blocking skills in players who are exposed to fatiguing conditions; to develop endurance in the muscles involved in vertical jumping.

Description: The coaches stand on two tables. One coach slaps the ball signalling the players to move. As the blocker gets close to the net, the coaches toss to hit the ball at the blocker. The blocker moves from one position to another , attempting to block the ball. The coaches should verbally correct any improper execution of blocking skills. Initially, the drill begins slowly and speeds up as the players improve.

Variations:

1. Have the blocker use a variety of movements, for example crossover, turn-and-run, or side-step, to increase the difficulty of the drill.

2. As the blockers become more proficient at blocking the balls hit directly at them, have the coach vary the location of the hit.

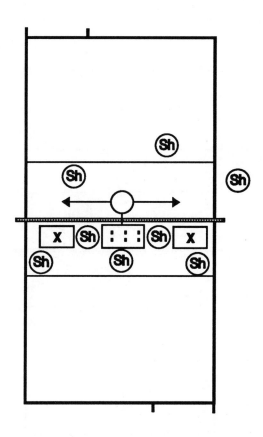

174 MULTI-PLAYER BLOCKING DRILL

Objective: To develop proper blocking techniques during one-on-one and double block situations, to enhance the proper body mechanics of the block, and to develop the off-blocker's ability to move from the net to the sharp-angle position.

Description: The drill begins with three blockers in the three front positions as pictured below (A-C). Three hitters stand on chairs across the net opposite the blockers (D-F). D in the left-front (#4) position spikes a ball cross court to Blocker A who is using a one-on-one technique. The middle hitter, E, spikes the ball cross court toward B, who also uses a one-on-one technique. Upon contact with the floor, B uses proper footwork to join A while D attempts to hit the hole in the block. At the same time, C comes to cover the sharp angle or tip. The same steps are performed to the opposite side as well.

Variations:

1. Incorporate additional defenders in the drill.

2. Move the position of the chairs to create blocking X's tandems or other combination.

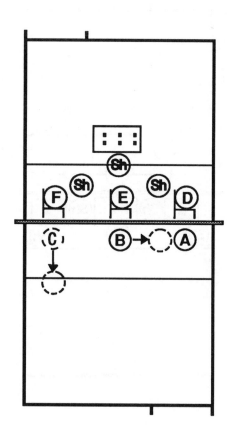

INDIVIDUAL SKILLS

175 SPIKER AWARENESS DRILL II

Objective: To train the blocker to be aware of the spikers approach angle and correct timing for blocking.

Description: Player A (the spiker) is positioned on the opposite side of the net from the blocker (B). The tosser (C) tosses a ball from behind player B to A, who approaches and spikes. The blocker must watch the spiker to get the visual cues needed to block the ball. The spikers quickly transitions off the net to spike again.

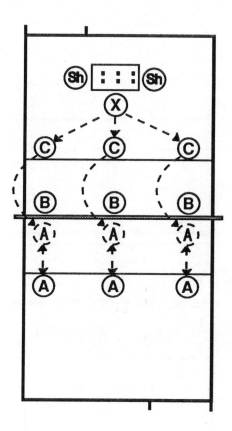

176 TEAM BLOCKING DRILL

Objective: To develop the ability to successfully team-block a spike; to develop the proper footwork and timing for 2-player blocking.

Description: A tosser tosses the ball to the coach who is standing on a table. The coach then spikes the ball directly towards the blockers. Blocker A in the center-front (#3) position moves to the right-front (#2) position as soon as the ball is tossed. Blocker B in the #2 position is aligned in accordance to the spiker's strongest spiking option. When A closes to create a two-player block, both players simultaneously leave the floor to intercept the ball. Both players return to the end of the line after completing the block.

Variations:

1. Have the tosser vary either the trajectory of the ball or the distance the tosser stands from the net to vary the resulting spike from the coach.

2. Perform the drill from the opposite side of the net.

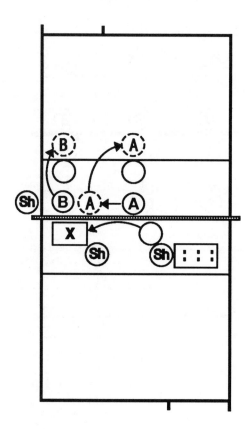

INDIVIDUAL SKILLS

177 ONE ON ONE BLOCKING DRILL

Objective: Perform proper blocking technique and timing.

Description: Players in the A line stand behind the attack line with a ball. On the opposite side of the net, positioned across from A, is a blocker line (B). Player A self tosses (1), approaches, and spikes (2). B positions, times, and correctly executes a block. Player A begins by spiking directly at B but progresses to spiking around the blocker.

Variation: A & B alternate spiking and blocking each time.

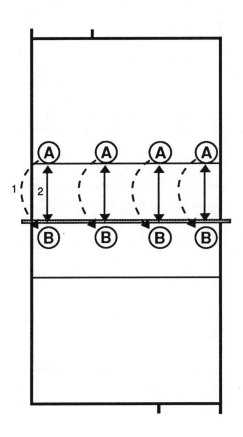

178 THREE POSITION BLOCKING DRILL

Objective: Perform proper blocking technique and footwork.

Description: Three hitters (A,B,C) stand behind the attack line with a ball. On the opposite side of the net, positioned across from A is a blocker (D) prepared to block. A self tosses, approaches, and spikes. As soon as D lands, B self tosses and D positions across from B. Again, as soon as D lands, C self tosses. Once D blocks against all three hitters, D returns to the end of the line and the next blocker positions across from A.

Variations:

1. The hitters can increase the rate at which they spike which forces the blockers to move into position to block more quickly.

2. The hitters can change the height and depth of the toss to increase the difficulty in timing the block.

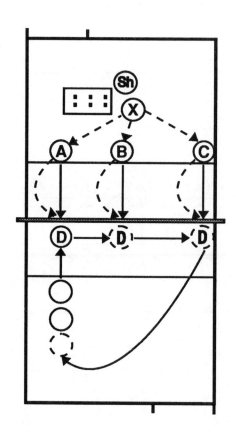

179 PEPPER BLOCK DRILL

Objective: To develop blocking technique and timing.

Description: Players A, B, and C are at the net, approximately 5 to 6 feet apart. On the opposite side of the net are two hitters with balls. Each hitter self tosses and spikes a ball alternately between two blockers, who try to form a two- player block. The hitters alternate spiking, the second immediately after the other has completed a spike.

Variations:

1. Increase the intensity and speed of the hits, forcing the pressure on the blockers.

2. All the hitters try to hit around the block teaching correct position of the block.

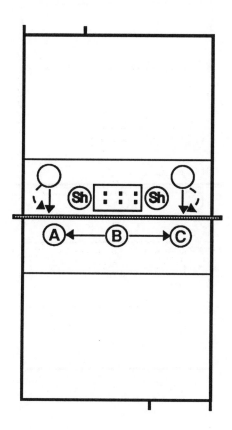

180 THE JOUST DRILL

Objective: Perfect the blocking technique and body control needed to be successful during a joust between two blockers.

Description: A tosses the ball on top of the net between players B and C. Both B and C try to block the ball to the floor. The player that was able to win the joust at the net goes to the end of that line.

Variation: Vary the height and position of the toss.

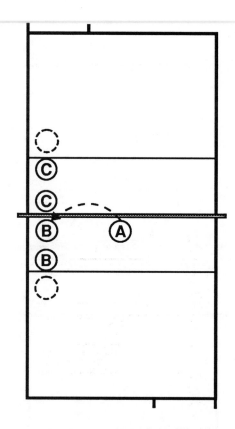

181 ONE-ON-ONE BLOCKING DRILL

Objective: To develop correct timing and individual technique required to successfully block the ball.

Description: The coach tosses the ball to player A. A spikes directly at blocker B. Using correct technique, B will attempt to block the ball. After each attempt to block, B and A both go to the end of their respective lines.

Variation: Blocker B stays at the net until a successful block has been performed.

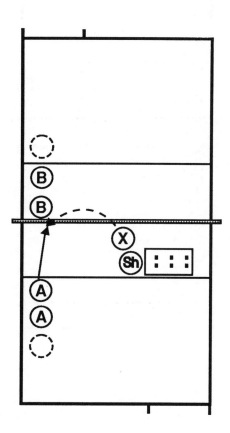

182 LIVE TEAM BLOCK DRILL

Objective: Develop the timing and coordination needed for a successful two-player block.

Description: The coach tosses the ball to A (1). Player B immediately moves to player C to form a 2 player block (2). A spikes directly towards the blockers. The spiker attempt to hit through the block. This is primarily for the blockers benefit so the spikers should hit progressively harder according to the success of the blockers. After each block the blockers and the hitter go to the end of their respective lines (3).

Variation: Run the drill in the middle of the net as well as the opposite side of the net.

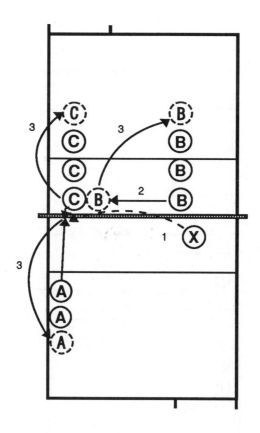

INDIVIDUAL SKILLS

183 BLOCK SWITCHING DRILL

Objective: To develope blocking endurance, team work and communication while blocking. Develop 2 player team blocking.

Description: A coach is located on both sides of the net at the center with shaggers and a ball cart. The drill begins with the coach tossing a ball to player A (1), who spikes against the opposing blockers, C and D (2). After the hit, A and B switch positions (3) and get into position to block. Player C backs off the net and the coach on this side tosses another ball for C to spike. After the spike, D and C switch positions and B now backs off the net to spike against the block. Players always exchanges positions after their side spikes.

Variation: Have the non-spike player cover the spiker in the event the ball is blocked. Have both players transition off the net and the coach toss to either spiker. The block must adjust accordingly.

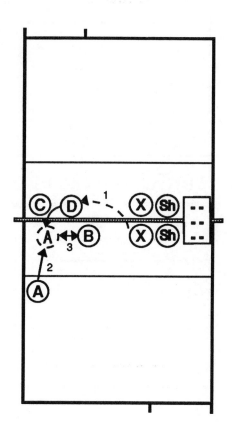

184 DOUBLE DOUBLE BLOCK DRILL

Objective: To train the 2 player block, communication, and team work.

Description: The coach starts the drill by tossing a ball to the setter (1), who sets a high ball to the left front (#4) position (2). Player A spikes the ball trying to hit through or around the two opposing blockers C and D (3). Immediately after the spike, the coach tosses another ball to the setter (4), who sets to the right front (#2) position (5). Player A sprints to right front (#2) position to spike a second set (6). Blockers C and D quickly move into position to block A. The same sequence is repeated with player B. After the sequence is repeated the spikers switch with the blockers.

Variation: Have the spiker also attack in the middle. Run the drill from right to left.

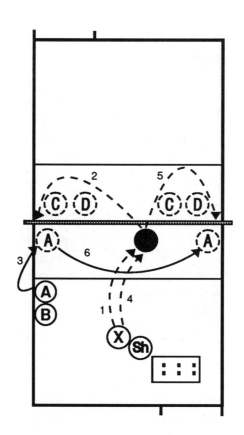

INDIVIDUAL SKILLS

185 HIT AND BLOCK DRILL

Objective: To train closing and set-up a 2 player block.

Description: Player a tosses to a setting/middle blocker B (1), who sets to A (2). Then A attempts to spike past the block formed by players C & D (3). Immediately after the spike, A sprints to the right front (#2) position and becomes the outside blocker. A and B now attempt to double block the opposing player E (4). Player E has tosse d a ball to middle blocker D (5) who sets to E (6). E spikes, then immediately replaces C (7), who has returned to the end of the hitting line (8) and the drill continues in this manner.

Variation: Have the spiker release and become the new middle blocker when forming the team block.

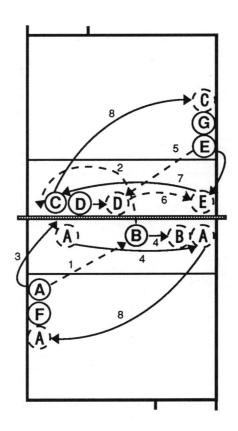

INDIVIDUAL SKILLS

CHAPTER 7

DIGGING DRILLS

186 GET BACK AND DIG DRILL

Objective: To develop the skills necessary to move forward and backwards on defense.

Description: The drill begins with one player standing ten feet away from the wall, facing the net. The coach assumes a position of similar distance from the digger with a ball. The coach initiates the drill by spiking the ball at the player (1) who digs it back to the coach (2). The coach self-sets the ball (3) while the player backpedals, touches the wall (4), and runs forward to dig another spike from the coach (1). This drill is continuous.

Variation: The digger begins by facing the wall, thereby having to turn on command to move to the ball and execute the dig.

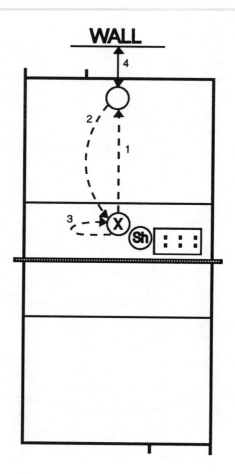

INDIVIDUAL SKILLS

187 DIG REACTION DRILL

Objective: To develop the digging skills and ability to read the spiker's angle.

Description: The drill starts by having two coaches spike the ball cross court to two diggers in their respective corners so that the players must move left, right, or forward(1,3). Players then try to dig balls up to the target (2,4). After a player plays one ball, the player then returns to the end of the line. The players should focus on watching the ball in relation to the coaches body.

Variations:

1. Conduct the drill down the line or to any area in which defensive backcourt players would be positioned.

2. Incorporate one or two blockers in the drill and have the diggers position themselves according to the positions of the spiker and the blocker.

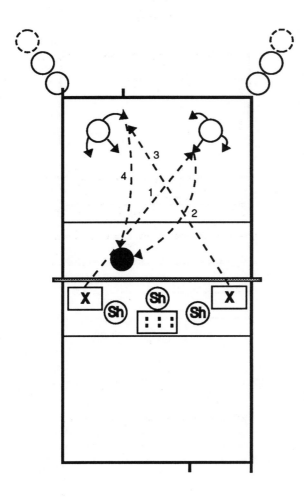

188 MULTI-CORNER SPIN DRILL

Objective: To develop digging skills and a willingness to hustle.

Description: The players form four lines facing center court as shown in the diagram below. The first two players in each line are given a ball. One player assumes a position in the center area equidistant from all four lines, facing line A. The first tosser in A initiates the drill by throwing the ball directly to the middle player. After the pass, the middle player must then turn towards line B. The first player in line B tosses to the middle player's left, using a roll the player makes the pass. The first tosser in line C throws to the middle player's right,and the tosser in line D throws a short which requires the middle player to dive. The middle player must recover from each pass and face the next line quickly. On each play, the middle player returns the ball to the tosser.

Variation: Have all passes tossed to one side of the middle player stress a specific roll, all passes short to develop the diving skills of the player in the middle, or all passes tossed straight to develop accuracy.

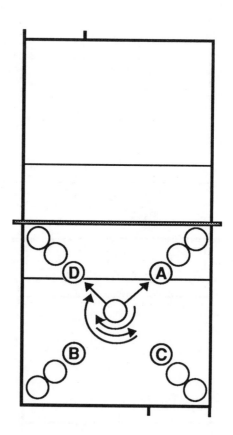

INDIVIDUAL SKILLS

189 CIRCLE DIG PASS DRILL

Objective: To develop the ability to dig the ball and introduce defensive positioning.

Description: The players form three lines facing the coach. The coach throws or hits a relatively hard spike to the first player in one of the three lines, who digs the ball and returns it to the coach. Once a player has received and returned a ball, the player moves to the end of the line. The coach continues to spike balls to all three lines.

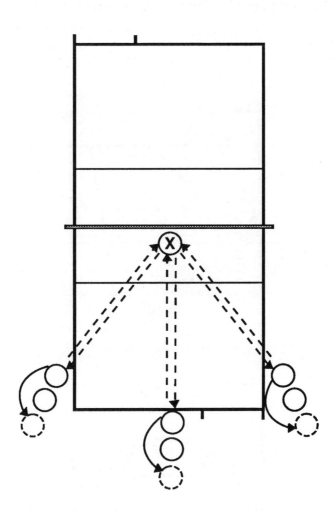

190 DIGGING ACCURACY DRILL

Objective: To develop the skills involved in digging accuracy

Description: The drill is initiated by having the coach spike the ball at the first digger (1) who is required to pass it to the first target (2). The players rotate clockwise from the digger to the target and from the target to the shagger. After the first ball is hit, the first shagger moves to the digging line.

Variations:

1. Vary the position of the coach.

2. Vary the position of the diggers.

3. Have the coach stand on a table and hit over the net.

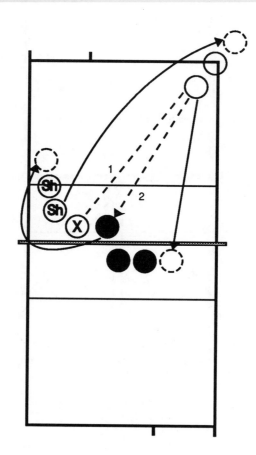

INDIVIDUAL SKILLS

191 DEFENSIVE MOVEMENT DRILL

Objective: To develop passing skills while performing various defensive movements.

Description: The players form a single line. The coach throws or spikes a ball (to the right, left, or straight) to a player (1) requiring the player to dive or roll on the floor after digging the ball back to the target (2,3).

Variation: The coach can use a soft toss instead of a hard spike or throw. The soft toss should be directed approximately three feet in front of the player. Additional soft tosses should be made just as the player is getting up off the floor.

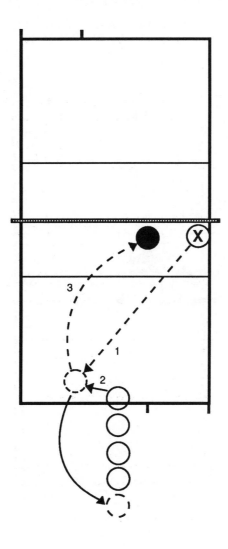

192 TWO FOR THE DEFENSE DRILL

Objective: To develop digging skills, positioning, and readiness on defense.

Description: The drill starts with hitters in the right-front (#2) position and left-front position (#4) on the same side of the court as a line of diggers as pictured below. Each digger moves one at a time to dig one line hit and then returns to the sideline to receive a cross-court hit. The hitters alternate attacking down the line and cross court.

Variations:

1. Have the diggers start at the attack line and adjust position prior to hit.

2. Have the players employ some method of emergency technique in order to increase the difficulty involved in spike recovery.

3. Locate spikers on the opposite side of the court standing on a chair or table.

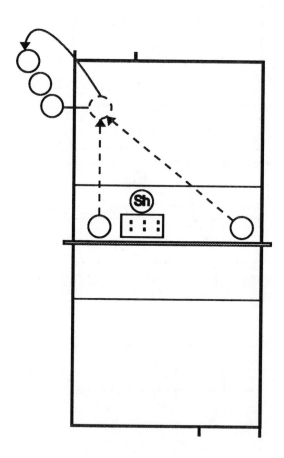

INDIVIDUAL SKILLS

193 RECOVERING AT THE NET DRILL

Objective: To develop the techniques for playing a ball out of the net and to improve reaction and concentration skills.

Description: The drill begins by having the coach, who is standing several feet from the net as shown below, hit the ball into the net (1). The first player in line (A) moves up to play the netted ball (2) and forearm-pass the ball to the coach (3). Once A hits the ball, A goes to the end of the line and the line moves up (4). The coach then hits the ball into the net again for the second player to recover. One ball is kept in play as long as possible. If the ball is not kept in play, the player should retrieve the loose ball and place it on the coaches hip until it is needed.

Variation: Move the line of players to different positions at the net.

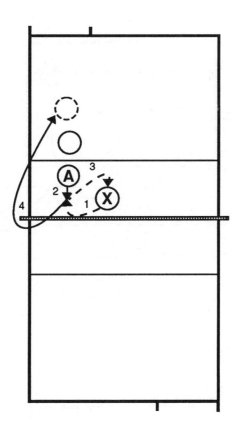

194 GO FOR TWO DIGGING DRILL

Objective: To practice the execution of an emergency technique after playing a ball.

Description: The drill is initiated with the coach tossing a ball to the left back (#5) position (1). The first digger in line (A) must run, dive, and attempt to play the ball back to the coach (2). As soon as the first ball is played, the coach then tosses a second ball to the right back (#1) position (3). Player A again attempts to play the ball to the coach (4). A then returns to the line, and B prepares to start the drill (5).

Variations:

1. Have the players play balls in different positions.

2. Have the players dig ball to a target in the setters area.

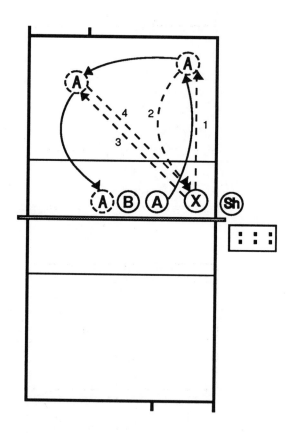

INDIVIDUAL SKILLS

195   DIG AND ROLL DRILL

Objective: To teach the skills involved in receiving spikes and executing emergency techniques.

Description: The drill begins when the coach spikes a ball to digger A. (1) As soon as A passes the ball. The coach immediately tosses or spikes a second ball at A (2), who must play it with the correct execution of an emergency technique (3).

Variations:

1. Conduct the drill from all backcourt defensive positions.

2. Have the coach stand on a table and spike the ball at the diggers.

3. Have the coach use a variety of attack positions.

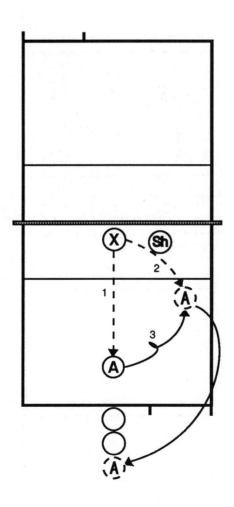

196 KEEP IT GOING DRILL

Objective: To develop the techniques for digging and executing emergency techniques to play balls.

Description: The drill begins by having a player who is in the right-back (#1) position dig a ball spiked down the line by the coach. The player then moves to dig a variety of shots on a non- stop basis: a ball tipped or spiked off the block (1), a deep spike to the left back (#5) position (2), a roll shot (3), a ball hit deep toward the sideline (4), and a tip (5).

Variation: Have the coach spike the ball from a table on the other side of the net.

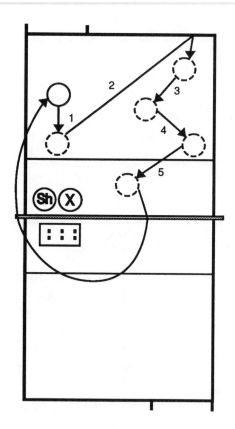

INDIVIDUAL SKILLS

197 NEVER SAY DIE DRILL

Objective: To teach the techniques involved in going to the floor after balls, and to practice emergency techniques.

Description: the drill involves three players assuming a position at least 15 feet to 20 feet from the endline. Starting with the player A on the left side, the coach tosses the ball so the players must execute emergency techniques after playing the ball (1,2). As A recovers, the coach tosses the ball to player B. As B recovers, the coach tosses the ball to the player C. A fast paced drill, this practice technique involves a large number of volleyballs and requires a good system of shagging balls.

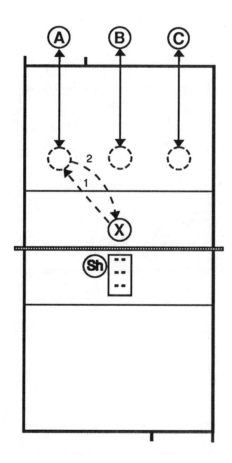

198 A WEAVING FIGURE EIGHT DRILL

Objective: To develop the defensive range of each player and to teach skill and emergency recovery techniques.

Description: The drill involves having players move constantly in a figure eight pattern to handle balls which are tossed to the players by the coach as illustrated below. The players must dig all balls to a target. Every player moving to play the ball goes inside. The player who has just completed playing the ball goes outside and cuts in over the baseline when the center court area is reached. After digging a designated number of balls, the three players (A, B & C) are replaced by the next group of three players to repeat the drill.

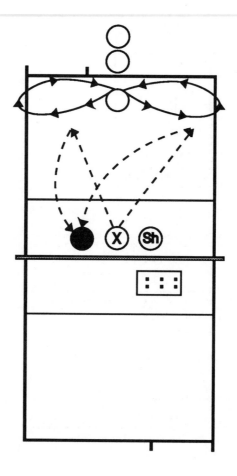

199 UP, BACK, AND SIDE-TO-SIDE DRILL

Objective: To improve defensive adjustment and directional responsibility.

Description: The drill begins with the coach spiking a ball to player A (1). A digs the ball to the target (2) then back peddles around cone #1. The coach immediately spikes to player B (3), B digs the ball to the target (4) and moves around cone #2. Then the coach spikes to player C (5) who digs (6) and backpeddles around cone #3. B is then spiked a second ball (3,4). B moves around cone #4 and the drill resumes with a spike to A again.

Variation: The tempo of the drill can be accelerated to the point that the players must execute an emergency technique while playing the ball.

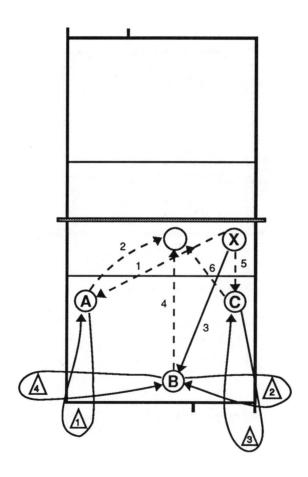

200 DIG SET DRILL

Objective: to develop defensive passing skills.

Description: The players form two lines and position themselves similar to playing doubles. The coach stands at the net and spikes or throws the ball at a relatively high velocity to player A (1), the first player in the line farthest from the coach. Player B runs up to the net from the other line (2), and player A digs the ball to B (3). B sets the ball back to the coach (4). After the first two players in each line take their turn, both players go to the end of the opposite line.

Variations:

1. The coach can vary the spiking or throwing position.

2. Player B could set the ball to the coach who could continue the drill with the next two players.

3. The coach could spike from the opposite side of the net.

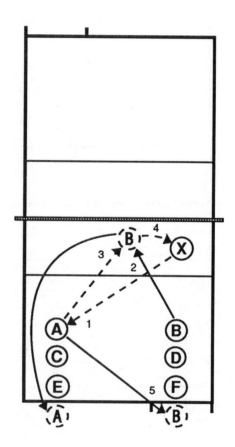

201 MULTI-PLAYER DEFENSE DRILL

Objective: To develop digging the seams and the open areas of the court.

Description: The drill begins by having players assume defensive positions on the court. The coach then hits balls randomly at the players, who return the ball directly to the coach off the dig. The coach concentrates on hitting the ball to the seams in the defense and to the open corners of the court.

Variations:

1. Conduct the drill to either the right or the left side.

2. Incorporate a setter in the drill who assumes the role of setting all digs to the coach.

3. Employ a lop shot to the line corner to force movement in the center-back area.

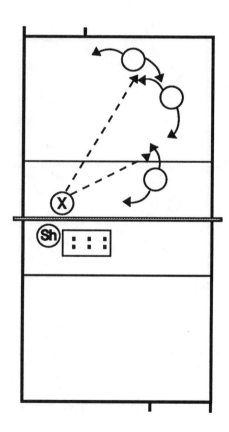

202 FOUR-PLAYER DEFENSIVE COVERAGE DRILL

Objective: To develop specific defensive skills and team movement techniques in relation to a point where an opponent attacks from various net positions.

Description: The drill begins with the coach hitting balls at the defensive players . The balls are hit to increase the player's range of coverage while simultaneously emphasizing proper court position. The coach controls the tempo of the drill and hits from a variety of positions along the net to simulate various court positions of an opponent's attack.

Variations:

1. Have the players employ different defensive formations.

2. Incorporate a setter in the drill to keep the second ball in play to the coach.

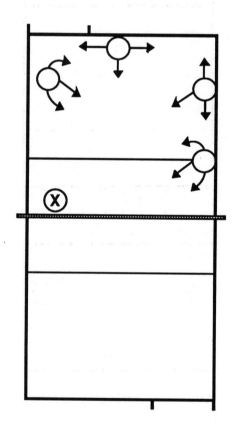

203 HALF COURT DIGGING DRILL

Objective: To improve emergency techniques, digging, and flow of play.

Description: This is a continuous action drill with the coach located on the same half court as the three diggers. The object is to keep the ball in play as long as possible. The coach spikes the ball at player A (1). A digs the ball (2) and then one of the other two players (B) must step and set the ball to the coach (3). The digger and the non-setting player should balance the court until the setting player returns to a digging position. The coach will continue to hit the ball. All diggers must be ready to set the ball, and communication among the players should be stressed to ease balancing and covering the court at all times.

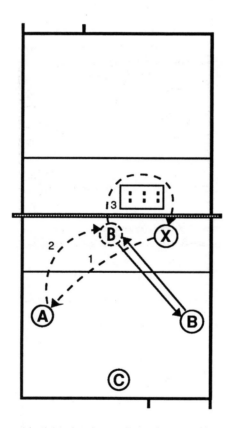

204 SPRINT AND CHASE DRILL

Objective: To develop the teamwork and communication skills necessary
  for running down a ball that is about to go out of play.

Description: The drill is initiated by having the coach slap the ball and
  toss a high ball outside the court (1). On hearing the slap, two defensive
  players (A and B) turn and sprint toward the ball (2). The player closest
  to the ball, in this case A, calls and passes it back to the second player,
  who is following (3). The player then passes to either target (4). Continue until ten balls have accurately been passed to the targets.

Variations:

1. Conduct the drill from the right- and center-back defensive positions.

2. Have the players who are manning the targets spike the ball, simulating
   a touch off the block.

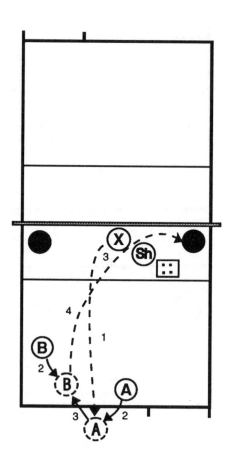

INDIVIDUAL SKILLS

205 DIG IT AGAIN DRILL

Objective: To teach individuals how to position themselves defensively and to develop the reaction and reading skills involved in digging.

Description: The drill employs two coaches, one in the left- front (#4) position and one in the right-front (#2) position. The coaches alternate spiking at two diggers on the other side of the net as shown in the diagram below. New diggers step in every two balls. The drill continues for a specific number of times.

Variations:

1. Incorporate blockers in the drill.

2. Have the diggers use an emergency technique for recovery after digging the spiked ball.

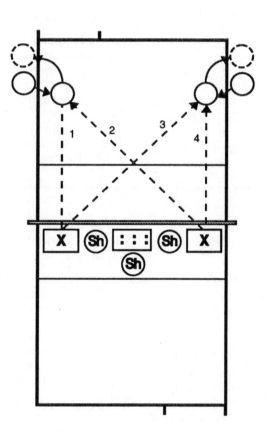

Other titles of interest from Masters Press:

The AVCA Volleyball Handbook

edited by Bob Bertucci

Twenty renowned volleyball authorities from around the country have contributed to this first official handbook of the American Volleyball Coaches' Association. Supplemented with charts, diagrams, and photos, this is an essential reference book for both coaches and players.

$17.95 * 352 pp * diagrams, charts, & photos

Kinesiology of Exercise:
A Safe and Effective Way to Improve Bodybuilding and Athletic Performance

Michael Yessis, Ph.D.

This is the most authoritative book available on how bodybuilding/weight training exercises can be performed for maximum effectiveness and safety. Written in a simple, easy-to-understand manner, the book also contains in-depth biomechanical and kinesiological analyses. Features approximately 70 exercises with explanations.

$17.95 * 224 pp * drawings and photos

Total Tennis Training:
Realizing Your Physical, Mental, and Emotional Potential

Chuck Kriese

Chuck Kriese, men's head tennis coach at Clemson University, explains the physical, mental, and emotional aspects of the game. Includes discussions of anaerobic endurance training, strength and flexibility training, nutrition, stroke production, technical skill development, injury prevention, and various game styles.

$17.95 * 224 pp * illustrated

A Practical Approach to Strength Training

Matt Brzycki

Responding to all those seeking a safer, more effective way to strength train, Brzycki examines all aspects of strength training - including specificity, plyometrics, high intensity training, and explosive training and offers information on creating personal workout programs.

$12.95 * 240 pp * illustrated

Five-Star Basketball Drills

edited by Howard Garfinkle

Here are 131 of the best conditioning, one, two, and three-player drills developed and used at Five- Star, the nation's premier basketball camp. A star-studded galaxy of coaches - including Bob Knight, Rick Pitino, Mike Fratello, and Mike Krzyzewksi - share the regimens that have proven successful year after year at Five-Star.

$12.95 * 256 pp * diagrams & photos

How to Jump Higher

James A. Peterson and Mary Beth Horodyski

A thorough explanation of how athletes can improve their vertical jump levels by following an organized program of muscular development. Includes information on strength training, plyometric drills, and the use of mental skills such as imagery to develop this crucial motor ability.

$12.95 * 144 pp * drawings & photos

Masters Press books, including all titles in the Spalding Sports Library, are available in bookstores or directly from the publisher by calling 1-800-722-2677